AFTER THE CRASH

AFTER THE CRASH

AMERICA IN THE GREAT DEPRESSION

JOHN RUBLOWSKY

CROWELL-COLLIER PRESS, NEW YORK, NEW YORK
COLLIER-MACMILLAN LIMITED, LONDON

PICTURE CREDITS

The Bettmann Archive, 12, 108; Culver Pictures, Inc., 3, 24, 37, 47, 54, 76–77; Franklin D. Roosevelt Library, ii–iii, 100, 117; Historical Pictures Service—Chicago, 20, 29, 34, 67, 130, 142; Las Vegas News Bureau, 129; United Press International, 6, 11, 16, 31, 39, 59, 74, 75, 88–89, 92, 94, 103, 119, 123, 124, 139, 151, 158, 161, 164–65, 173, 176

The Macmillan Company, 866 Third Avenue, New York, N.Y. 10022
Collier-Macmillan Canada Ltd., Toronto, Ontario
Printed in the United States of America

10 9 8 7 6 5 4 3 2

CONTENTS

PRELUDE

1

Everything seemed to stop. Factories shut their doors;
banks failed; farmers could not sell their produce and
left crops to rot in the fields; paper fortunes disappeared;
businesses closed, and mortgages were foreclosed; cities
and towns were bankrupt and could not pay salaries for
those who worked for them. Unemployment grew, and
there was no work. The economy of the United States
ground to a painfully slow crawl. The depression had
descended upon the country, and a shocked and bewildered people braced against the crisis.

How did it happen? Why did the richest economy the
world had ever known collapse so suddenly? What were
the causes? Who was responsible? Where could blame be
placed?

Even today, almost forty years after this catastrophe

struck the nation, economic and political experts are not certain. All they can say for sure is that everything stopped, that the economy collapsed. One day America was enjoying unprecedented prosperity. The next day the nation was gripped by depression.

Some cite a failure of confidence, of spirit or nerve, as the underlying cause; some blamed overproduction while others pointed to underconsumption as the real culprit. Some went right out of this world to place the blame. They tried to explain the economic crisis in terms of cyclical disturbances on the surface of the sun. Still others described the depression as the debt the world had to pay for the resources and wealth squandered in a disastrous World War I. Many of these factors undoubtedly played a role in bringing about the Great Depression that held the nation in its grip throughout the 1930s, but the real reasons are probably much more complex and may never be completely understood.

Where shall we begin the story of this depression whose effects are still being felt today? The root causes were deep and can be traced to sources in the very history and nature of mankind. We can see beginnings in the Industrial Revolution, which transformed the world in a little more than 200 years; and we can go back even further in time. Yet, we must begin somewhere. A good starting point, used by many economists and political analysts, can be Europe's descent into World War I in 1914. This war had a profound effect on the American people and their economy, establishing patterns in both areas that remain to this day.

In 1914 the United States was a large country, and no one doubted that it was rich. Blessed with almost un-

Before World War I America was primarily a rural nation

limited natural resources, having one of the most extensive belts of fertile farmland in the world, protected from European war and intrigue by large oceans, boasting a vigorous and growing population, America had apparently no limits to its potential. Yet in 1914 this potential was barely making itself felt on the international scene. America was a provincial country far from the seats of power. London was the financial capital of the world, and Paris was the cultural center. Study in a German University was a must for any ambitious young American who hoped to make a mark in medicine, philosophy, or science.

America was primarily a rural, agricultural nation with the bulk of its population living on farms or in small towns. Although the seeds for a great industrial complex had been sown, this factor was still of only minor international significance. Our technical progress was not highly considered and our popular culture—our music, movies, comic strips, and dance—had not yet Americanized the leisure life of the world. Americans admired European books and art, and the "latest" thing in practically every field was of European origin.

Our foreign policy, except for the regulation of the almost casual plunder of Latin America, was nonexistent for all practical purposes. Militarily, our armed forces were no larger than necessary to make the western hemisphere safe for American speculators. Since our neighbors were, for the most part, undeveloped and disorganized, this level of preparedness placed little strain on our national resources. Our financiers, except when they had to borrow money abroad, were totally involved with domestic affairs.

With World War I the position of the United States in world affairs changed overnight. For one thing, this was the most destructive and expensive war the world had ever known till this time. It consumed men and materials on a scale that dwarfed all earlier conflicts. In the beginning, the war had an unsettling effect upon America that was reflected in a sharp, though temporary, setback to the economy. At the time, America was a debtor nation whose expansion was financed in large part by European banks. Repercussions of the European war were felt in the American financial structure.

Then, in an increasing flood, came war material orders from the Allies. American industry and agriculture quickly tooled up to meet this demand. American business found itself with an unlimited and profitable market for everything it could produce. Steel and dynamite, potatoes and cotton, boots and trucks were consumed or destroyed on the battlefields of Europe as fast as we could deliver them. Between 1914 and 1917 America paid off its entire debt to Europe, estimated at $7,000,000,000 and for the first time in its history became a creditor rather than a debtor nation.

When America entered the war in 1917 Allied purchasing power and credit was at the point of exhaustion, but the slack was taken up by a new source of credit, the United States government. The "seller's" market continued stronger than ever. In response American industry and business performed miracles of organization and expansion. In our factories the machines never stopped, and every factory hand worked overtime. Every farmer cultivated all the land he could manage and then some while accumulated capitol grew steadily in the banks and counting houses.

As for the war itself, it had no great physical effect upon the nation. No bombs fell in America, and no battle was waged on our soil. We had suffered heavy casualties— some 126,000 American servicemen died in the war—but neither our military nor economic strength had been greatly affected.

For American business the victory was even more dramatic. During the past four years industry had witnessed and participated in an extraordinary phenomenon. Even with 4,000,000 of its best young men in uniform, the productivity of America had risen to incredible heights. Our economy had outfitted an enormous army from scratch and kept it lavishly provisioned and equipped. We

*As soldiers returned from the war to compete for jobs, the
American economy experienced a sharp—but brief—decline*

had supplied the Allies with unheard of quantities of food, clothing, metal, fuels, weapons, and ammunition. We had built billions of dollars worth of airplanes, tanks, and trucks and had feverishly constructed the largest navy in the world.

More important, the American economy had performed this miracle of production with no serious strain. During the war there had been "wheatless days" and "gasless Sundays," but even these deprivations were mostly for propaganda effect. There were no acute shortages in America except for sugar, and this shortage was principally the result of speculators and war profiteers who had cornered the market. The average American, both at home and at the front, was better fed, better clothed, and better housed, for the most part, than ever before. For the people of Europe, the war had been a disaster that left wounds that have never fully healed. For us, it was more like a stimulating adventure that left the United States the strongest of the great powers and provided a revealing hint of what we might accomplish.

Immediately after the Armistice, the American economy experienced a sharp decline. Orders for war material stopped and soldiers returned to the civilian economy to compete for jobs. This condition, however, proved to be temporary. A new attitude had developed across the country—especially in the business community—that the setback had to give way to boom. This feeling was based on fact; it reflected a knowledge that practically every person in America shared.

We remembered the astonishing activity that the war had stimulated. We also knew that the nation was none the worse for this spurt of economic expansion. Our economy was better off than ever before. The industrial complex had grown enormously, and people saw no reason why it should not be utilized for peace with the products of industry used for something better than killing the Hun. There was no reason why full-steam production should not continue.

We had all the essential raw materials. We had great industrial capacity. We had skilled workers and highly trained technicians. We had inventive brains and organizing ability. We had energy to spare. Why not open the throttle and start things rolling?

Ideally the economy of a nation should produce all the things that its people need and want to the limit of its productive capacity, which was exactly what had happened during the war. All that was necessary now was to shift the production from the materials of war to the needs of peace. It was very simple and not at all difficult to understand. But the American economy was not ideal. It was a patchwork quilt of outmoded traditions, prejudices, vested interests, and a complex financial structure all under the influence of a philosophy of no governmental controls or restraint. The prime moving factor in this complex was profit, not the needs of the people. Automobiles, for example, were not produced because people needed them. They were produced in order to make a profit for the manufacturers. Should this profit cease, production would also cease whether or not people still needed the automobiles.

The fundamental laws that regulated this laissez-faire economy defied analysis. Indeed, the history of the Industrial Revolution was marked by recurrent crises. Suddenly, prices collapsed. People stopped buying, and the economy would falter in its progress. Eventually things generally straightened themselves out, and the economy would lurch ahead once more. The economists argued bitterly about the causes for these setbacks, but they could never agree, not even among themselves.

One thing, however, was definitely known, and on this point almost all of the experts agreed. The industrial system never maintains anything approaching full capacity just to supply the needs of the population. There has to be some dramatic outside stimulus. War, of course, is one of these factors. The industrial machinery of a nation always responds to the demands of armed conflict. Even fear of war may provide the necessary push.

In time of peace, the conditions for capacity production are more complex and much more subtle. Such a boom, economists of the time felt, could be created by a feeling on the part of the public that tomorrow is certain to be better than today. If such a feeling is broad enough and reaches a larger enough portion of the population, things begin to move.

When people feel secure about their future, they buy the things they need or the things they simply have always wanted—it may be a used car, a new suit of clothes, or that little place in the country where one can get away for weekends. This demand stimulates manufacturers to produce more. They add extra shifts and install more machines, employ more men and buy more materials. Each expansion in the process brings more money into the economy, and the more money available the more people buy, causing more expansion, more purchasing power. The results are cycles that spiral upward so long as the public remains optimistic.

AFTER THE CRASH   10

This was the outlook that dominated American business after World War I. There was no need for governmental control or regulations. Leave business alone and business would take care of everything. There would be jobs and abundance for all. "A chicken in every pot and a car in every garage," was the cry around which the country rallied. All the country needed was confidence—confidence and optimism.

If America had anything after the war ended in 1918 it was these two qualities. Hadn't we beat the enemy without half trying? Hadn't our economy supplied the Allies with more war materiel than the world had ever seen? Wasn't this same economy intact and ready to produce even more for an abundant peace?

The answer in all cases was, yes!

After a sharp recession in 1919 the economy began an upward spiral of production and abundance that appeared, for a time, to have no limits. The new decade (1920) saw the triumphant election of a Republican president, Warren G. Harding, who promised a return to "normalcy"—interpreted by the business community as the absence of governmental regulation. For the rest of the country, normalcy meant a repudiation of Wilsonian idealism. America had had enough of European entanglements and wanted no part of Wilson's League of Nations or any other foreign commitments. America wanted to forget the war and enjoy the abundance of its own economy.

By the time Warren G. Harding was elected in 1920, America wanted to forget the war and enjoy the abundance of its economy

Illegal saloons flourished in spite of the high moral purpose of Prohibition

It would be difficult to attempt to recapture the atmosphere that prevailed in America at the start of this fateful decade. American society was such a maze of contradictions and opposed tendencies and directions that it is almost impossible to describe. The country, for example, was under Prohibition. The Volstead Act had been passed in 1919 making it illegal to manufacture, sell, or transport any alcoholic beverage. The law reflected a majority opinion in the country and was supported by large numbers throughout the land.

The high moral purpose of Prohibition could not be denied, and as such it represented the last gasp of the Puritan tradition which had been dominant in America. But, as was soon made painfully clear, the moral life of a nation was all but impossible to regulate through legislation. People continued to buy and sell liquor even though to do so was against the law. The law was ignored. Bootlegging, the illegal manufacture and smuggling of liquor, became a national industry on a scale that presupposed wholesale corruption of police and government officials. Illegal saloons and cabarets where liquor was sold flourished throughout the country in open defiance of the law.

Prohibition had split both major political parties as it did the nation and become the most controversial and talked about issue in politics. In the face of the unprecedented prosperity of the twenties, a subtle change occurred in the outlook of the nation. Soon, the "drys" were identified in the popular mind with "country preachers," farmers, old maids, and professional kill-joys. The "wets" became handsome young men and pretty girls. They were jolly good fellows and sports. They were dashing rum runners and gallant police officers who acted out an exciting charade. Breaking the law became a game and hardly anyone considered the consequences— the widespread corruption of the police, the establishment and growth to power of hoodlum empires, the general moral corrosion. For this moral corrosion and open flouting of the law was not confined to rum runners and bootleggers. It spread until it engulfed important segments of all levels of society. The Harding administration was barely two years old when it revealed the first hint of scandal. Harding, a genial Ohio politician with little experience in national or international affairs before his election, did not understand economics at all, according to his own testimony. He relied upon advisors who came without exception from the ranks of big business. They assured the President that big business was not only sound but also had wonderful plans for the nation's future if he would only give sufficient leeway.

Behind the imposing facade of the administration which could point to the very moral Charles Evans Hughes, the very efficient Herbert Clark Hoover, and the very rich Andrew Mellon in key positions, there was careless management and corruption. Harding not only did nothing to regulate business, but he also allowed his advisors a free hand to use the nation's resources for personal gain.

Harding's career was cut short by a brief illness and he died in San Francisco on August 2, 1923 under what many considered questionable circumstances. The President, however, died at the height of his popularity, and the nation was genuinely sorry. For weeks the newspapers and magazines were full of eulogy. National leaders in all phases of business, politics, and religion sang his praises. The special train that brought Harding's body east was greeted along the route with what *The New York Times* described as "the most remarkable demonstration in American history of affection, reverence and respect."

Calvin Coolidge, the Vice-President, assumed the office of president. His administration was barely inaugurated when the scandal that had been accumulating under Harding broke upon the nation. The Harding administration, it was discovered, had participated in an unprecedented looting of national resources. The scandal reached a climax with the notorious Teapot Dome revelations.

The federal government had set aside certain oil-rich areas of public land as a fuel reserve for the Navy. On April 7, 1922 jurisdiction over the reserve was transferred from the Navy Department to the Interior Department by an order of President Harding. Under this authority, Secretary of the Interior Albert B. Fall leased a large tract in the Teapot Dome district of Wyoming to the Sinclair interests and another tract in the California reserve to oil tycoon Edward L. Doheny.

A Senate investigation into the matter revealed questionable procedures in the transaction. As a result, Secretary of the Navy Edwin Denby resigned, and criminal proceedings were instituted against Interior Secretary Fall, Attorney General Harry M. Daugherty, and oilman Edward Doheny. Interior Secretary Fall was convicted and served time in a federal penitentiary. Daugherty and Doheny, however, were acquitted, though the Attorney General was compelled to resign by President Coolidge. The nation was in the midst of a surge of prosperity and no one wanted to rock the boat. The scandal was passed

Secretary Fall and Harry Sinclair, two of the principals involved in the infamous Teapot Dome scandal of 1926

over even though it created an enormous sensation, which the newspapers of the day exploited to the hilt.

One of the most remarkable aspects of the case was the apathy of the public. Although there was considerable interest in the melodrama, there was no public outcry of either rage or indignation. No one seemed to care about the thievery, and the whole sordid mess was quickly hushed up.

Despite the scandals, Calvin Coolidge was elected in 1924 by a huge majority. The nation was obviously satisfied with the way things had been going for the past four years and saw no need to change. Economic conditions had improved steadily and showed every sign of continuing on this happy course. This condition was attributed to the basic Republican policy of giving business free rein. The moral aspects of the Harding scandals carried little weight, and the public saw no reason why the same party, the same leaders, should not continue in power.

Actually corruption in government was no more than a reflection of a mood and attitude that seemed to affect almost the entire country. In many respects the 1920s was a decade of both unprecedented prosperity and profound hypocrisy. The prohibition laws, for example, were openly flouted, and a sizable proportion of the population indulged in a "get rich quick" orgy that asked no questions about the means through which wealth was acquired. Speculation became the pastime of not only the wealthy industrialists, but of an ever-growing part of the population. The stock market was the new Eldorado where everyone could get rich.

This development, in itself, indicated one of the major changes in the attitude of the middle-class American in this decade. Before the 1920s only wealthy men and speculators played the market. The small investor put his money into the safest bonds he could buy, and even this transaction was accomplished only after the most careful deliberation. If the small investor had asked his trusted banker for a low-price common stock with speculative possibilities, the banker would have reminded him of his responsibility to his wife and children and kept an eagle eye on his account forever more. Such activities were for the rich or the irresponsible.

Gradually, this attitude changed—was changed may be more correct. American business instituted an all-out, many-sided campaign to interest the public in common stocks. Some of these moves were direct. The public utilities, for example, hired high-pressure salesmen and promoters to persuade the public to buy their securities. Manufacturers distributed stock to their employees, often at favorable prices. More people began to own stocks, and with ownership came interest in stock market activities. Even if a man owned only a single share, and that half paid for, he was likely to check the financial pages of his daily newspaper to follow the movements of A.T.&T. or to see what G.M. was doing.

Another contributing factor was the change in banking policies and procedures. Where the old-fashioned banker might have recommended a gilt-edged bond in which the investment is protected by an actual lien on a company's assets, his new-style successor or competitor did not hesitate to praise a common stock that might not have a good dividend record but was "certain to go up." Often he had such securities at hand and could pass them over the counter like so much currency. As the prosperity of the 1920s rose toward its peak, such practices became the rule rather than the exception.

The public education was finished off by the press. Each year, each month, stock market news occupied more space in the newspapers and magazines. Business reports crept out of their usual place in the back financial pages and shared the front page with the latest crime. Personalities from business and finance made the headlines and the society pages. Market "operators" were the new purveyors of glamour, and they became popular idols alongside movie stars and athletes.

The stock market became a kind of national game, a

wonderful lottery in which nobody lost. Stocks, many speculative and unsound, were bought by an ever-widening part of the population. The speculative nature of the market was further exaggerated by the widespread practice of buying securities on "margin." What this meant, simply, was that the buyer paid only about 25 per cent of the price of the stock. Seventy-five per cent of the price was extended to him in the form of credit. The buyer could, of course, be asked to cover the margin—to pay the remainder of the cost of the stock. So long as stock bought one day could be sold the next at a higher price, no one really worried about the margins.

In the face of this buying pressure, stock market prices soared—they doubled, tripled, and quadrupled, and there was no ceiling in sight. Everyone made money and the economic leaders waxed ecstatic over the prospects. All this activity had its effect upon the general public. It seemed that willingness to take a chance was the only thing one needed to become wealthy. And the opportunity to take this risk was made as simple and as painless as possible.

You bought stock on margin and waited. When the stock went up you sold out at a profit and bought more shares. These also went up. There was no end to the process. The old laws of economics had been repealed, and America had entered into an era of permanent prosperity. Prosperity did not need explanation. It did not matter how it came about just so long as it remained and continued to grow.

Nor was this prosperity the monopoly of the leisured classes or the Republican Party. Getting rich was the right of all and within everyone's reach. A method to achieve

ANOTHER MODERN IMPROVEMENT

—Orr in the Chicago *Tribune*.

A 1929 cartoon illustrates the prevailing feeling of optimism when it seemed that the old laws of economics had been repealed and America had entered a period of permanent prosperity this end was advocated by John J. Raskob, chairman of the Democratic National Committee:

If a man saves $15 a week, and invests in good common stocks, and allows the dividends and rights to accumulate, at the end of twenty years he will have at least $80,000 and an income from investments of around $400 a month. He will be rich. And because income can do that, I am firm in my belief that anyone not only can be rich, but ought to be rich.

Here, then, was one of the fundamental changes that occurred in the American society during this fateful decade. Overnight, America turned from a conservative society guided by the old-fashioned principles of thrift, self-reliance, and independence to a nation of speculators. Farmers and tradesmen, craftsmen and factory workers, secretaries and professionals all became infected with the speculative fever. The decade saw a bewildering succession of land booms and investment trusts all of which promised "quick money," but offered little in the way of safeguards.

Another fundamental change occurred in the financial organization of the economy. Almost imperceptibly a shift had come about in economic control from the industrial capitalism of an earlier day to finance capital. What this meant was a change in emphasis. The primary purpose of industry was no longer the manufacture of products, but the making of money. This era saw the sharp growth of holding companies that took control of industry from the hands of the industrialists. The holding company permitted a small group of stockholders to gain control over widely scattered empires of interlocking or even loosely related interests. The men who devoted their lives to the development of a manufacturing plant would find themselves suddenly a small and powerless part of an enormous corporation that had been created for speculative purposes. From then on their actions would be controlled by the financiers who had the key to the structure. Their plants became interlocked into a huge financial network the needs of which alone determined policy.

Still another basic change was developing in marketing and distribution. The twenties witnessed the growth and proliferation of the national chain store. This development paralleled the growth of the holding companies and the mergers that they stimulated. All of these developments merely reflected the vigorous thrust of the new economy. Centralized industry, followed by centralized marketing and distribution complexes, made every American city, every hamlet, every region part of a web that fit snugly into the newly emerged national pattern for making, selling, and distributing commodities.

The economy of America had never been so highly integrated. The farm, the village, the county seat, and the large cities had been wrapped up in the consolidations and mergers that were spurred by finance capital. As never before, the great financial combines called the tune. They not only controlled utilities and industry, but merchandising and distribution had also fallen under their sway.

The effects of this consolidation changed the structure of the population of America drastically. At the beginning of World War I wage and salary workers made up little more than one-half of the working population. By the mid-1920s this portion had risen to more than four-fifths. America had changed from a nation of small, independent farmers, craftsmen, and merchants to one where the overwhelming majority depended upon wages for their livelihood. An interdependence unknown in old-fashioned America had become the economic fact.

Along with these developments came an even more basic change in the structure of American society. Actually, this change was part of a worldwide agricultural revolution. All over the world agriculture was in a state of flux. Merger and consolidation ruled the farms just as it did the public utilities and industry. The small, independent farmer who supported a self-reliant household became a thing of the past. Small-scale farming was no longer economically feasible. Mortgages were foreclosed, and the land became concentrated in fewer and fewer hands. This process still continues. Today, the farm is most likely to be a huge industrial facility with an enormous investment in machinery and equipment completely beyond the means of the independent farmer with limited land and capital.

The industrial farm became increasingly a specialized producer of a particular commodity. Like the industrial worker or the merchandiser, the farmer also became dependent upon a centralized economy. The wheat farmer, for example, bought his bread from the local A.&P.; the cattle rancher bought steak and hamburger from the same source after it had been processed and packaged by one of the big packing companies. The produce he grew or raised became his "cash crop." He did not produce anything else. It did not pay.

As a result, the small, inefficient family farm was doomed. Throughout the twenties there was a steady attrition of such holdings. As long as the economy prospered, this situation was not cause for serious concern.

The displaced farmer merely packed up his things and moved to the city where he found a good-paying job in a factory or mill that provided him and his family a more comfortable living than they had ever experienced down on the farm. His old 100 acres, first broken by his father or grandfather, became part of a vast holding that was worked with engineered efficiency. Per capita production of the farm operators soared, and each year saw fewer farmers producing more vegetables, meats, grains, and

Throughout the twenties the small family farm gave way to the engineered efficiency of vast holdings

other agricultural products in a curve of steadily mounting efficiency.

During the 1920s the American economy changed from a provincial, rural, agricultural one into an industrialized, highly centralized type, with efficient utilization of resources promising an ever-expanding standard of living for all. In the year 1928 many responsible American leaders and thinkers believed that poverty was well on the way to being abolished. More people were provided with more of the good things of life than ever before and this prosperity seemed certain to reach even the meanest levels of our population. It was a triumph of unrestrained capitalism. Free enterprise, with a minimum of governmental regulation and interference, had demonstrated its capacity to fulfill the needs of the people.

There were, of course, voices raised in protest to the "get rich quick" attitude which appeared to grip the nation. There were also economists and analysts who warned that the unprecedented prosperity of the 1920s was constructed on a bed of quicksand—on dangerously expanded credit, on the squandering of irreplaceable resources that had to be paid for in the long run.

These voices were either ignored or ridiculed. The voice of the booster was heard in the land. He saw a lovely vista of growing prosperity stretching away as far as the eye could see. There was corruption in both government and business, but this, after all, was only "human nature." What if a bit of the wealth of the nation was looted? There was more than enough for everyone. And if a little corruption was necessary to keep things rolling, there was no one to begrudge this price. Prosperity was here to stay; that was all that mattered.

THE HOOVER ADMINISTRATION

2

The "roaring twenties" was a Republican decade. It began with the election of Warren Harding to the presidency in 1920 and came to a close with the administration of Herbert Hoover. Between these two Calvin Coolidge reigned after assuming office upon the death of President Harding. Coolidge also won his own term in the election of 1924 when he defeated his Democratic opponent. Almost six years as president, however, was enough for Coolidge and he told the nation on August 2, 1927: "I do not choose to run for president in 1928." His successor was Herbert Clark Hoover, who was nominated by the Republican Party and elected to office by a landslide majority.

The twenties, then, were dominated by the Republican Party, and this fact, in itself, was something of a contradiction. The political philosophy of this party advocated efficiency and economy in all phases of government and a minimum of governmental interference in the economic and industrial affairs of the nation. It was basically a conservative philosophy. Yet the society as a whole was anything but conservative.

Radical and sweeping changes were shaping new styles and patterns in every area of American life. In industry centralization and consolidation completely transformed the structure of the economy. In business a speculative fever had replaced the old-fashioned traditions of thrift, hard work, and self-reliance. Living styles had changed drastically. Jazz, a new music, erupted on the scene, and a generation of "flappers" scandalized their elders. Old moral standards seemed to have disappeared. Prohibition was the law of the land, but the law was openly flouted everywhere. America was on a spectacular binge, and there was no law that could put a damper on the party.

Yet, in the face of these extravagant social and economic developments, the Republican administrations remained isolated, for the most part, from the popular currents. The government was conservative in the truest sense of the term. Its principal goals were economy and efficiency, and its ideal was "the less government the better." After the early scandals of the Harding administration, the Republican leaders settled down to a remarkably restrained role in conducting the nation's affairs.

The outstanding feature of the Coolidge administration was precisely this aloofness from the affairs of business and industry. Coolidge said, "the business of America was business," and prudently left business to the businessmen. The Coolidge administration worked hard to control government spending and to lower taxes. The reductions favored industry more than any other segment of the economy, and a high protective tariff helped further by protecting industry from foreign competition. Regulatory agencies of the federal government became institutions for the assistance of business. Everything was geared to further the expansion of industry and business, and, the administration felt, this expansion could be best accomplished through economy and noninterference.

Coolidge's policy of limited governmental participation in economic affairs put him in firm opposition to many reforms advocated by Congress. Although the economy was booming, there were numerous troubled areas. Agriculture, for example, was in a state of crisis throughout the decade. The small, family farm simply could not compete in a free market, and each year more such farms failed. In order to alleviate farm conditions, the McNary–Haugen farm relief program was passed by both the House and the Senate. Coolidge, however, vetoed the bill and it was never enacted. For him, the farm problem was a passing thing that would work itself out without governmental assistance.

The President also tried to stop a bill that provided a bonus for veterans of World War I. Public sentiment for the bill was so strong, however, that Congress finally passed it over the President's veto.

In foreign affairs, Coolidge reflected the general public outlook by pursuing a policy of nonentanglement. His administration was not markedly isolationist and did its best to maintain and develop good relations with other countries. Coolidge was also a strong advocate for international peace and general disarmament but attempted

URSULA: "Is my nose shiny, Dearie?"
LAMBERT: "No, but your right knee is dusty."

A generation of flappers began to scandalize their elders by drinking, smoking, and wearing short skirts

to accomplish these ends without troublesome treaties or pacts. Coolidge unsuccessfully urged adherence to the World Court but bowed to public sentiment in keeping America out of the League of Nations. He favored naval disarmament as a step towards both peace and economy. The most notable event in the administration's foreign policy was the signing in 1928 of the Kellogg–Briand Pact to outlaw war.

On the whole, Coolidge's administration was marked by lack of serious crises, the absence of any spectacular or dramatic leadership and, most important, an exhilarating growth of prosperity. His aloofness from and lack of positive policy in regard to the economic life of the nation was simply a postponement—a sweeping under the carpet of serious problems. This lack of over-all policy, together with his complacent encouragement of the speculative boom in the stock market, produced serious predicaments for future administrations. The consequences of this neglect settled upon Herbert Clark Hoover, who was inaugurated as President of the United States on March 4, 1929.

In many respects, Herbert Hoover was the most capable and imaginative of this Republican triumvirate. Certainly, he came to the office with the broadest national and international experience in both industry and government.

He was born in West Branch, a small Iowa town. He was the second of three children of Jesse Clark and Huldah Minthorn Hoover, both Quakers with a long American Quaker ancestry. His father was a blacksmith and his mother was a schoolteacher. His father, however, died when Herbert was six years old, and his mother died two years later. He was brought up by an uncle, Henry John Minthorn, a doctor living in Newberg, Oregon.

Deciding early on a career in engineering, Herbert Hoover enrolled in the first freshman class of the newly opened Stanford University in California on October 1, 1891. Not wealthy, Hoover had to work his way through school and supported himself by doing typing and operating a laundry service and newspaper route for his fellow students. During summer vacations he worked as an assistant with a state geological survey in Arkansas and with the United States survey in California and Nevada.

After graduating from Stanford in 1895 Hoover worked for a time as a laborer in California mines in order to gain practical experience. Later, he joined the staff of Louis Janin, a mining engineer of San Francisco. The experience gained in this position brought young Hoover to the attention of Bewick, Moering & Company, an English engineering firm with extensive interests throughout the world. He was put in charge of their mining properties in Australia in October 1897 and became a partner in the firm in 1901.

He remained with the company until 1908 when he

Herbert Hoover (right) rides with Calvin Coolidge (left) on their way to Hoover's inauguration in 1929

established his own engineering company. His work with the firm had taken him to projects in Europe, China, Africa, New Zealand, and Australia, but Hoover had maintained a California residence throughout this period. His own company had its headquarters in London, and, except for periodic visits to America, Hoover spent the eighteen years before World War I abroad.

As an American citizen living in England at the outbreak of war in 1914, Hoover organized and served as chairman of an American committee in London that helped secure passage home for more than 100,000 United States tourists and visitors in England and Europe. Thus began a career in public service that was to carry Herbert Hoover to the presidency of the United States some fourteen years later.

When America entered the war in April 1917, Hoover returned home where President Wilson appointed him United States Food Administrator in August of that year. Hoover's broad experience in both industry and public service soon made itself felt. He proved to be an extraordinarily efficient administrator. During his tenure in office Hoover organized the United States Grain Corporation, Sugar Equalization Board, and Food Purchasing Board, agencies that, under his direction, handled over $8,000,000,000 in supplies for the United States and its Allies. During the critical year from July 1, 1918 to July 1, 1919, Hoover's food administration furnished 18,500,000 tons of food, more than three times the normal American export to the Allies and the famine areas of Europe.

After the Armistice Hoover was put in charge of a vast international program of war relief to prostrate Europe.

Establishing headquarters in Paris, he coordinated the distribution of food and material aid on an unprecedented scale. These operations spread over thirty European countries where Hoover not only expedited the distribution of food and materials but also established a relief program for 10,000,000 undernourished and homeless children. His administration of these programs was both efficient and effective, and they are credited with saving millions of lives in war-torn Europe.

Hoover's administration of America's vast war-relief programs brought him into international prominence. This American Quaker engineer, who was born in the humblest circumstances in the nation's heartland became a world hero. After the Republican victory in the 1920 election, President Harding appointed Hoover to the important cabinet post of Secretary of Commerce. In this capacity, Hoover undertook the reorganization of the department on the basis of voluntary cooperation among commercial, agricultural, industrial, and labor interests. When the Harding administration was rocked by scandal, no hint ever touched Hoover in either his public or private affairs.

He retained his cabinet post throughout the Coolidge administration and was nominated by the Republican Party as their presidential candidate in 1928. Actually, Hoover's reputation as a result of both his wartime duties and his postwar work in European relief had singled him out as presidential potential. As early as 1920 he had been considered by leaders of both parties as a possible candidate. Hoover was, however, a registered Republican, and his political career was irrevocably allied with this party. Among Republicans in 1920 Hoover was con-

A Chicken *for* Every Pot

THE Republican Party isn't a *"Poor Man's Party:"* Republican prosperity has erased that degrading phrase from our political vocabulary.

The Republican Party is *equality's* party—*opportunity's* party—*democracy's* party, the party of *national* development, not *sectional* interests—the *impartial* servant of every State and condition in the Union.

Under higher tariff and lower taxation, America has stabilized output, employment and dividend rates.

Republican efficiency has filled the workingman's dinner pail—and his gasoline tank *besides*—made telephone, radio and sanitary plumbing *standard* household equipment. And placed the whole nation in the *silk stocking class.*

During eight years of Republican management, we have built more and better homes, erected more skyscrapers, passed more benefactory laws, and more laws to regulate and purify immigration, inaugurated more conservation measures, more measures to standardize . and .increase production, expand export markets, and reduce industrial and human junk piles, than in any previous quarter century.

Republican prosperity is written on *fuller* wage envelops, written in factory chimney smoke, written on the walls of new construction, written in savings bank books, written in mercantile balances, and written in the peak value of stocks and bonds.

Republican prosperity has *reduced* hours and *increased* earning capacity, silenced *discontent*, put the proverbial "chicken in every pot." And a car in every backyard, to boot.

It has *raised* living standards and *lowered* living costs.

It has restored financial confidence and enthusiasm, changed *credit* from a *rich* man's privilege to a *common*

utility, *generalized* the use of time-saving devices and released women from the thrall of *domestic drudgery.*

It has provided every county in the country with its concrete road and knitted the highways of the nation into a *unified* traffic system.

Thanks to Republican administration, farmer, dairyman and merchant can make deliveries in *less* time and at *less* expense, can borrow *cheap* money to re-fund exorbitant mortgages, and stock their pastures, ranges and shelves.

Democratic management *impoverished* and *demoralized* the railroads, led packing plants and tire factories into *receivership*, squandered billions on *impractical* programs.

Democratic mal-administration issued *further* billions on mere "scraps of paper," then encouraged foreign debtors to believe that their loans would never be called, and bequeathed to the Republican Party the job of *mopping up the mess.*

Republican administration has *restored* to the railroads solvency, efficiency and par securities. .

It has brought the rubber trades through panic and chaos, brought down the prices of crude rubber by smashing *monopolistic rings*, put the tanner's books in the *black* and secured from the European powers formal acknowledgment of their obligations.

The Republican Party rests its case on a record of stewardship and performance.

Its Presidential and Congressional candidates stand for election on a platform of sound practice, Federal vigilance, high tariff, Constitutional integrity, the conservation of natural resources, *honest* and *constructive* measures for agricultural relief, sincere enforcement of the laws, and the right of *all* citizens, regardless of *faith* or *origin*, to share the benefits of opportunity and justice.

Wages, dividends, progress and prosperity say,

"Vote *for* Hoover"

Hoover's 1928 victory was a triumph for the Republican policies of the previous eight years

sidered a progressive and as such could not stand up against the old-line conservative sentiment reflected by both Harding and Coolidge.

After Coolidge had bowed out as the Republican candidate for 1928, Hoover emerged as the outstanding figure in the party and won the nomination easily. He proved to be a good choice. In defeating Alfred E. Smith, the Democratic nominee, Hoover polled 5,500,000 more votes than did Coolidge in the previous election. The victory was a triumph for both Hoover and the Republican policies of the past eight years, although some observers attributed Hoover's victory in part to religious prejudice. Alfred E. Smith, governor of New York, was a Roman Catholic—a factor of no small importance in the campaign and vote.

What kind of country did the new President inherit from his predecessors? On the surface, things could not have been better. The nation was in the midst of booming prosperity. All over the land more people were working, buying and saving than ever before. Factories were operating at full capacity, the stock market was soaring, and new price levels were reported after almost every trading session. The world was at peace, and there was nothing on the horizon to mar the picture.

Of course, there were some troublesome spots in the economy. Agriculture, especially as it concerned the small farmer, continued in a state of crisis; the coal mining industry was in a bad way as was the textile industry—coal mining because of increasing competition from other sources, mainly oil and water power; and textiles from growing foreign competition. Some observers felt that credit in the stock market had reached dangerous levels, and there were those who said that the working people of America were not getting a full share of the general prosperity. Speculative stocks, they pointed out, had risen from an average of 100 at the beginning of the decade to more than 400, but wages had only gone up from an index of 100 to 112 in this same time.

There were other sore points, but these were looked upon as no more than minor irritants in an otherwise serene and optimistic picture. Hoover, the American public was confident, would put things aright in short order. America had never had a president like this. Hoover was a dynamic, vigorous leader. He was accustomed to dealing with astronomical sums of money. Coolidge had left business alone; Hoover would help business to fulfill its destined role of creating permanent national prosperity. Hoover was also a Quaker humanitarian who had demonstrated his concern for the poor and hungry of the world through practical and concrete action. He would be more than a match for any problem that might confront the nation.

Actually, the most pressing problem that the new administration faced was not economic at all. It was a crisis in morality. Prohibition laws were being flouted on more levels every day. Bootlegging became a national disgrace along with a parallel growth in the power of organized crime. Hoodlum empires had been consolidated during this period along the lines of industrial centralization, and their strength and influence appeared to be reaching a critical point. Entire municipalities had been corrupted by underworld organizations. Here, too, Hoover was looked upon as the savior. No scandal or hint of wrongdoing had marred his career. The Quaker

"You can't have any, Fred, you gotta drive the car."

Prohibition laws were flouted on more levels every day

engineer would surely clean up the mess that was corrupting the country.

These deficiencies, of course, were no more than petty annoyances, weeds that needed to be pulled out before they grew too big. On the whole, the country was sound and showed every indication of becoming sounder. Manufacturers and merchants all over the nation were announcing new heights in both production and sales. Jobs were easy to find, and raises, though they did not come often for factory workers, kept pace with the economy in most fields. The college graduate hardly had time to roll up his diploma before he was bombarded with attractive offers from a dozen competing companies. Business was growing. Men, especially skilled and educated men, were needed everywhere. The honest worker, for the most part, was comfortable if not affluent. The bootlegger, the bond and stock salesman, the nightclub owner, the speculator was, if not wealthy, well on the way to achieving this status. The new administration promised even more, for all economic curves were pointing up, rising ever more steeply towards no one knew what heights.

On the lighter side, things were even more rosy, if such a situation were possible. Tunes were gayer and the dances wilder. The young men were handsomer and more dashing, and girls were prettier. American morality, once strait-laced and puritanical, was rapidly shedding its thorns. Happy was the man or woman who was young in 1929—and all the world felt young.

Even beyond the borders of the United States, the world was getting along fine. The menace of communism did not appear so dangerous any longer. America had shown that capitalism, pure and unadulterated, could provide amply for more people than any other economic system ever tried. In Russia the communists appeared to believe it too. At any rate, they had given up trying to promote world revolution and had exiled Leon Trotsky, its leading advocate. Now they were importing American machines and American engineers to help them become as productive as America.

The world looked up to America as the richest, strongest, and most influential nation in the world. The most pressing question was: "How did we do it?" To find the answers, delegations of German, English, French, Italian, and other experts came to study our methods and tech-

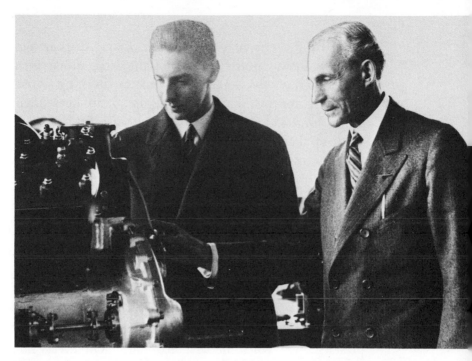

Henry Ford (right) explains the intricacies of a motor to Prince Nicholas of Rumania (left)—one of the many foreign visitors who came to learn about the American economy

niques. Our factories and industrial plants played host to a steady stream of foreign visitors who came to learn. They wrote books about the American economy, full of praise. All over the world, people read our literature, adopted our fads, danced to our tunes, and sang our songs. They called Hoover the "Great Engineer" and employed American experts to straighten out their financial affairs.

A *Pax Americana* had settled over the world, for prosperity and good times had flowed over our borders and were soothing people everywhere. Even poor, defeated

Germany was enjoying a good year. Latin America was thriving. It was peaceful, too, for the local strong men could borrow any amount of money in New York ostensibly for public works and use it to keep their armies loyal and their restive populations quiet.

All of these things helped set a tone to which all of America responded. These things made even the humblest citizen very proud and very happy, but what made them proudest of all was the new self-respect that all Americans enjoyed. Class lines, for example, had all but disappeared. People dressed alike and played alike. The rich and poor saw the same movies, listened to the same radio programs, and cheered the same athletes. In Newport beach "cottage" socialites rubbed elbows with bootleggers, athletes, and jazz musicians.

This, then, was the America that Herbert Clark Hoover presided over when he assumed office. On every side there was growth, activity, and orderly turmoil. Cities all over the country were expanding, resulting in a spectacular building boom. Soon there would be a new high office for every business and for every family, a new little house.

A year earlier, in his acceptance speech at the Republican convention, Hoover had soberly announced that the conquest of poverty was no longer a mirage: "We have not yet reached the goal, but given a chance to go forward with the policies of the last eight years, we shall soon with the help of God be within sight of the day when poverty will be banished from the nation." No one doubted that Herbert Hoover was sincere in this opinion or that he believed that his administration would accomplish this goal.

BLACK
THURSDAY

3

What goes up must come down was not necessarily so. The old common-sense adage had been repealed—at least as far as the stock market was concerned. Since the end of World War I stock prices had climbed steadily for ten years. When President Hoover took office on March 4, 1929 the ceiling to the long bull market was nowhere in sight. (In stock exchange parlance a "bull" market is a period of rising prices. A "bear" market is one in which prices fall.) The steady climb in stock prices reflected and paralleled the unprecedented growth of American industrial capacity on all levels. Most Americans looked upon the stock market as an index pointing the way to an era of permanent prosperity.

There was no reason why they shouldn't have. Learned economists, government officials, and financial experts reassured them continually. Professor Irving Fisher of Yale University, for example, spoke knowledgeably about a "permanently high plateau" of economic well-being—the consequence of the miracle of American productive and organizational abilities. Professor Charles Amos Rice of Ohio State concurred in this opinion and announced that the nation had, indeed, entered a "new era."

One observer compared the ship of state to a great ocean liner plowing majestically through the sea. Here, for all to admire, were the spacious decks, the polished brass, and the spotless linen in the dining room. Below, the softly purring engines were a miracle of modern engineering, working so efficiently that we were hardly aware of their presence. Everywhere aboard this wonderful ship was a feeling of confidence. All was well, and the ship would carry its passengers to their destination safely and comfortably.

Although they did not intrude upon the bridge, the new era economists assumed that the ship was in the hands of competent officers. They were not certain, however, who those officers might be. Certainly it was not the government. Its practical abdication from the economic affairs of the nation had created a vacuum. This vacuum was filled, in large part, by the most reckless and irresponsible elements of business—by self-seeking interests, greedy speculators, and unprincipled financiers who had no objective other than making themselves as rich as possible.

There was never a sharper contrast or more distance between the engineers and technicians whose admirable efficiency and inventiveness had created the industrial giants and the cynical and reckless financiers who controlled them. The electrical industry, for example, had been making dramatic, even spectacular progress. The Steinmetzes and Teslas had steadily improved the quality and lowered the cost of electricity. They had designed marvelously complex grids that provided electricity to the smallest hamlet of America and had developed innumerable useful devices and appliances. On the technical level their plants and generating facilities were models of efficiency and often social enlightenment as well.

But directing everything were the financiers. In theory, a public utility was a trust which was supposed to charge only such rates as would give them "a reasonable return on their investment." In practice, they had developed into lucrative speculative ventures. To protect themselves from regulation, the power magnates bribed public officials, corrupted newspapers, and employed batteries of lawyers to conceal their maneuvers in a legal tangle. Some of these utilities, like the Chicago empire of Samuel Insull, became so tangled that they were never completely straightened out. Insull, himself, was prosecuted on charges of fraud after the collapse of his holdings. Although he was vindicated, Insull died a pauper.

Everywhere it was the same. On one side was the real and admirable developments of the technicians, on the other were the financiers. Steel companies and chemical plants, clothing manufacturers and retail chains, packing houses and canneries—the entire economic apparatus of America was in the hands of financiers whose sole objective was to make money. Everything had been subordinated to this goal.

Yet, the financiers were not completely to blame. They were aided, abetted, and encouraged by a speculative fever that gripped the entire country. Everyone with a little spare cash became a gambler. Everyone wanted to get rich, and the easiest road to this end was through the stock market. As we have already seen, vast portions of the public poured their money into securities, oblivious of the consequences.

There was no Securities and Exchange Commission to pass on the soundness of a stock; there were no limits to credit; and there were no regulations. People wanted stocks, and the need was satisfied. Almost any stock issued was gobbled up in the hope of striking it rich. Many of these securities were worthless. A Curtis Wright Aeronautical Company, for example, sold out an issue of 20,000,000 shares in early 1928 within weeks after it was put on the market. The company's principal asset, it later turned out, was an employee named Curtis Wright. The real aviation stock was Curtiss Wright Corporation, but aviation stocks of any kind were the glamor issues of the day, and speculators were quick to exploit this fact. The Seaboard Airline, as another example, was actually a railroad and had nothing whatever to do with aviation. The name, however, attracted thousands of investors.

Credit had become such a monster that by September 1929 more than $8,000,000,000 had been extended in the form of brokers' loans that covered margin purchases of securities. Still the prices continued to climb, but by this time the value had become mostly paper—stock prices represented the greed, hopes, and dreams of investors and had almost nothing to do with real value as represented by the assets and earning potential of a particular company or firm. That the market was heading toward a fall was already obvious. Many conservative economists and government figures issued warnings, but they were ignored. Reality could not compete with a dream in progress.

Actually, a more concrete warning had already been sounded. It happened in the Florida land boom, which began in the early 1920s, reached a peak in 1925, and collapsed in the spring of 1926. In many respects, the entire economy of the United States was repeating this prophetic experience.

The Florida boom was, strictly speaking, hardly a Floridian affair. The entire episode was organized, engineered, and promoted by northern speculators. Like most booms, the Florida land bubble had its origin in fact. For several years land values in this semitropical state had been rising. There were good reasons for this rise. Florida was sparsely populated and had a superb climate, free of the winter rigors of northern states. Railroads and highways had opened up extensive areas that were almost inaccessible before, and more and more people were visiting this "winter playground" for vacations.

This was the trigger. Here was a huge, empty, undeveloped state with legitimate assets—a perfect opportunity for making money fast. How? Buy some property, or better still, buy an option—an agreement to buy property at a specified price within a specified time. Sit tight as the price goes up. Sell at the right moment and pocket your profit. It was that simple. Soon it seemed that everyone wanted to get into the act. All over the country people invested in a Florida "plot," generally associated with a development hopefully described as a "winter paradise" or another "playground for the rich."

Prices soared under the buying pressure. Real estate in

the business section of Miami—a town with fewer than 75,000 permanent residents at the time—sold for as much as in downtown Manhattan. 100-by-50-foot "building" lots ten miles outside the city sold for $30,000. The circle spread, engulfing dreary swamps, tidal flats, grass wilderness—everything became part of a development. People paid for land they had never seen, often for land that did not even exist. As long as they could sell their interest again a few weeks later at a profit, it did not matter.

It was a classic example of a panic-boom cycle. It began, like most booms, with a legitimate rise in value that ignites the initial excitement. Next came the speculators who gained control of most of the available land. They began beating the drums to the age-old lure of quick profits and easy money. They made the prospects enticing enough to interest a wide circle of buyers. The boom began. Every rise in price attracted more buyers. The circle widened. At this point, the original speculators who engineered the boom began to take their profits and quietly creep away. They were no longer a factor in the boom or its eventual collapse. The process had been transformed into a bubble that continued growing until there was no longer enough substance to keep it intact. At a critical point, when selling in order to take a profit exceeded buying, the bubble burst and reality took over from the dream. Suddenly, people realized that an acre of swamp or sawgrass wilderness was simply not worth the price that had been paid and the boom ended—more swiftly than it began.

By the spring of 1926, the Florida bubble had burst. The inflated prices for land came tumbling down with a crash. Florida was left littered with half-finished hotels and

Many of those who lost money in the Florida land boom repented only of not having invested sooner

flimsy bungalow colonies. Forty years later, one could still find weathered signposts in sawgrass fields in the midst of nowhere that pointed to imaginary Buena Vista Boulevards and Sunshine Lanes.

Such was the optimism of the time that the most important lesson people learned from this experience was not the danger of speculation. Those who had put their money into a Florida swamp at $25,000 an acre did not feel that they had made a mistake. They felt that their mistake had been in not doing it soon enough.

With extraordinary unanimity, everyone—government, public, and press—concluded that the Florida panic had been no more than a silly episode without relevance to the national economy. There was no lesson to be learnt here and people were soon looking elsewhere to invest their money in the hopes of getting rich quick.

They did not have far to look. The stock market beckoned invitingly. The "market" was no longer a mystery. Everyone was an expert. The public flocked to buy stocks and the companies that issued securities made it as easy as possible to obtain them. A favorite device was the stock split. A company whose securities sold at $100 a share would announce that it would issue four new shares for every one old share. The reasons the management gave were that it wanted "a broader base of ownership" or "wider distribution." The actual reason was more likely that the split made it easier to sell the company's stock because the price per share became cheaper. The effect of such an announcement was inevitable. Prices would rise. The old share jumped to $120 and the new, when issued, sold at $30 or more.

There were all kinds of stock—common and preferred,

voting and nonvoting, class A and class B. One utility even issued a mysterious security that paid no dividends at all, but was purported to be even more valuable than ordinary stock that did. The issue sold out almost as soon as it became available.

Most of this trading was done on "margin." The buyer paid for only a portion of the stock he bought, usually around 25 per cent. The broker advanced the rest by borrowing from banks. There was, of course, a limit to the amount of credit that could be extended in this manner. By early February 1929 the banks were running out of money and there was little left in the credit pool for brokers' loans. Yet without credit which permitted buying stock on margin, stock prices could not be maintained, let alone rise, and the whole financial structure of the economy depended upon rising stock prices.

Banks had already extended more than $6,000,000,000 in brokers' loans, which meant that the price level of the stock market was shakily supported. Even a slight drop would compel the banks to call in their money from the brokers. The brokers, of course, would pass the onus back to the margin speculators. Many of these would not be able to produce the cash on short notice. The brokers would then have to sell the speculators' holdings before their value fell too far below what had been lent on them. The forced selling would further depress the market and trigger another chain of the same unpleasant consequences.

This was the situation in February of 1929. Credit had reached the limits of normal banking resources and the Federal Reserve Board, the governmental agency that regulated banking, was worried enough about the condition to issue a warning. There was little more that the board could do in the year 1929. Theoretically, it was supposed to act as a central government bank to regulate interest and discount rates in the banking industry. In fact, however, its powers were feeble. It had no authority with which to take any drastic or far-reaching actions. It could, however, raise the interest rate at which it loaned money to member banks, in an attempt to stop the spiral of stock market prices. This action it proposed to do. The board announced that it would raise the rate, then 5 per cent, to member banks, which, in turn, would raise their interest rates on brokers' loans and so tend to reduce margin trading by making it more expensive.

A shudder ran through the financial community at the prospect. Everyone knew that market prices were inflated. They also knew that anything that might affect the confidence that kept prices buoyed could have disastrous results. The financial powers exerted all the pressure that they could bring to bear upon the government to forestall the move. They succeeded, at least temporarily. No one wanted to rock the boat—not President Coolidge who wanted to retire in a blaze of glory, not the new president who wanted to begin his administration on a suitably high and optimistic note, and certainly not the large financial interests that had constructed loosely bound empires resting on a foundation of high stock prices.

The speculators won. The discount rate was not raised and the market celebrated the good news by staging a sharp upturn in prices that more than made good the losses that followed the initial news.

Actually this was no more than a temporary postponement. The situation was becoming more critical as the insatiable demands for credit grew. In late March, after the new president had been inaugurated, the Federal Reserve Board banks instituted a policy of refusing all loans on securities. Little was said about the measure in public, but the policy was having its effect. Money was getting tight, and traders were becoming nervous.

By the last week in March, this undercover nervousness had become intense and had spread to the trading public. The exchange was swamped with selling orders, and prices dropped. The interest rate on call money—the form of credit used to back margin purchases in moments of crises—rose swiftly from 12 to 20 per cent. Even more serious, it could not be obtained even at this price. The Federal Reserve banks had cut it off at the source. On March 26 the market fell sharply on a flood of sell orders. By noon thousands of margin calls were going out over the wires. Traders were being sold out. Nervousness was turning to fear and fear could easily lead to panic.

The Hoover administration did nothing, but another focus of power became very active. Charles Edwin Mitchell had just negotiated a merger that made his National City Bank the largest in the country. Early in the afternoon of that critical March 26, he announced that if the Federal Reserve banks would not provide call money, the National City would. It committed its vast resources to the support of the market.

The effects of this announcement were swift and dramatic. It meant that the biggest, most powerful bank in America was backing the market. It meant, more significantly, that the biggest bank had tapped sources of credit that could not be cut off by the Federal Reserve Board. The market recovered almost immediately. By closing time the morning's losses had been wiped out in a rush to buy that lifted the day's trading to 8,246,740 shares, record high for the period.

Many of the smaller traders had been frightened out of the market by this spasm, but they soon flocked back. There was an unlimited supply of credit again to support margin accounts. The new source was the enormous amount of money that had accumulated during the past twenty years in the treasuries of the great corporations. They were quite willing to lend it out as call money at 8 or 9 per cent. This rate was more than it could earn anywhere else, and there was little risk involved. Call money was exactly what the name implied, it could be called back at a moment's notice.

Some of the more realistic financial experts viewed this new source of credit with alarm. Credit obtained through banks was at least semiresponsible. It would not be withdrawn at the first signs of danger. Nonfinancial corporations had no comparable responsibility. Inevitably, their credit would be called back at the very first sign of trouble.

This resort to corporate funds to further inflate the market was described by *The New York Times* as "credit procured from unusual sources . . . which will fail in the end." No one seemed to care or even to pay any attention to such predictions. By the end of May money was available in ever-increasing quantities. Brokers carried any amount of stock on margin, and prices continued to rise. The market was in the final stages of a classic boom, and the public was growing more and more excited and exhilirated by the prospects.

The summer of 1929 was probably the wildest, most

reckless period in American financial history. Stock prices soared far above the dangerous levels of the winter before, and with them soared the hopes of America. The pessimists were finally silenced—overawed, perhaps, by the continued rise of the market. Any warnings were buried in the press and ignored by the public. Hoover was in the White House and all was well with the world. Indeed, the President seemed sincerely convinced that his would be the honor of leading America and the world into a new age of peace and prosperity.

The country was living in a dream—a technicolor, wide-screen, stereophonic fantasy. More people were actually far richer—at least on paper—than they had ever hoped to be. Periodicals devoted much of their advertising space to sable coats, yachts, limousines, penthouse apartments, gold-plated plumbing, and the like. These luxuries were within reach of everyone who had the key, and the key was the stock market.

It was still climbing. Securities were selling at prices out of all proportion to either their yield in dividends or the position of the company itself. The old rule that a stock was worth ten times its net earnings became a joke. Financial experts insisted that they were worth at least fifteen times their earnings. Actually many were selling at twenty, thirty, and even forty times this figure. Some speculative favorites had never paid a dividend. Radio Corporation was one of these, yet the value of a share bought at $94.50 in March 1928 had gone up in eighteen months to $505.

Early in September the market broke slightly, and a few overextended traders were wiped out. The market, the experts assured the public, was experiencing nothing

CADILLAC

*A*MONG General Motors cars, the
Cadillac, with its famous 90° V-type eight-cylinder
engine, offers the supreme combination of beauty,
performance and appointment—the ultimate in fine
car luxury at prices from $3295 to $7000

The Cadillac of today is a consum-
mate expression of fine car crafts-
manship—modern in engineering,
and in its intimate harmony with
present day ideals of smartness and
refinement.

Three epochal engineering developments make it still more notable for
performance, ease of operation and
safety—the new Duplex-Mechan-
ical four-wheel brakes that meet
the requirements of modern motoring; the new Syncro-Mesh silent-
shift transmission that renders gear
shifting a well-nigh subconscious
operation; and crystal-clear non-
shatterable Security-Plate glass in
all doors, windows and windshields.
The engine is Cadillac's greatest
single contribution to motoring—
the famous ninety-degree V-type
Eight. For the finest of fine motor
cars this engine is without equal
in performance, long life and economy of operation.

Coachwork is by Fisher and Fleet-
wood interpreting in the modern
vogue, Cadillac's traditional beauty.
Adjustable driver's seat in enclosed
models, mohair or broadcloth up-
holsteries, oxidized silver hardware
with escutcheon plates inset with
Catalin stone, exquisite vanity cases
and smoking sets, torchere type
rear quarter lights—all contribute
to the patrician richness and lux-
urious travel ease associated with
the name . . . Cadillac.

GENERAL   SPRING
MOTORS   SHOWING

*Americans continued to speculate because the stock market
seemed to be the key to the luxuries advertised in the periodicals
of the time*

more than a brief breathing spell. A breathing spell, however, was precisely what the market could not afford. It implied a slowdown, an opportunity to stop and think. In the light of cold reason, things did not look good at all.

All through that September, stock prices continued to drop slightly. There was nothing spectacular about the sag—no panic, no rush to sell. There appeared to be very little reason for worry. Industry after industry reported record production and sales for the third quarter of 1929. But the market drifted slowly downward despite individual days when it rose and the old fever showed itself again. The astute traders were quietly selling out. It would take several more weeks before their nervousness was communicated to the public.

On October 14, the market broke sharply. The break was attributed to an incident that occurred in Boston. The Boston Edison Company had applied to the Massachusetts Public Utility Commission for permission to split its stock four to one. On Friday, October 11, a rumor began to circulate around the Boston exchange that this permission was denied. At closing the price of the stock had dropped from $440 to $360.

This, however, was not the end of the affair. Not only did the commission refuse permission for the stock split, but it also initiated a rate inquiry on grounds that a power company with $100 par (or face) value stock selling above $400 might be taking too much money out of the public pocket. On the next Monday, October 17, the stock plummeted to $300—a loss of nearly one-third of its value three trading days ago.

This incident alone may not have had any marked

effect upon the market, but it occurred in conjunction with a series of weakening influences. The more astute traders, as we have already seen, were quietly disposing of their common stock. Another factor was the failure of the Hatry Group, a huge English investment trust that had poured vast amounts of money into the American stock market. The failure forced the trust to sell its American holdings in order to raise cash to meet its European obligations. Thus another strain was placed upon the market.

The fact no one wanted to face was that the market could not absorb strain in its overextended state. A feeling of apprehension gripped the financial centers that week. Everyone knew, or at least suspected, that the gerrymandered trusts, the holding companies, the utility empires, indeed, the entire industrial complex of America had been intertwined in the financial wheeling and dealing that had characterized the stock market over the past ten years. It was a gigantic structure built on greed and dreams. How long could it stand up?

The nation held its breath, waiting. On October 18 and 19 the market continued to sag, and investors were beginning to feel the first stabs of fear, if not panic. Sensational rumors flew around the board rooms. The decline was attributed to a mighty battle between competing interests —it was nothing more than a cleverly manipulated bear raid. But it was more than that. The market was not behaving as if a bear raid was in control. Selling was too broad, too general. Orders were coming from too many places to be the work of any individual trust or even combination of trusts.

What was the government up to during this dramatic

week? President Hoover had gone to Detroit to participate in a jubilee celebrating the Golden Anniversary of Light. The gala meeting was organized by Henry Ford to honor the invention and inventor of the incandescent lamp and to celebrate the accomplishments of industry and technology during the past fifty years. It was a bright affair attended by notables from all branches of industry and business. President Hoover delivered the keynote address for the occasion, congratulating the inventors and industrialists who had led America to its present "high plateau of prosperity." This was probably the last pleasant weekend that Herbert Clark Hoover would enjoy as President of the United States.

On Monday in New York the market opened on an ominous note. President Hoover was cruising on a steamer down the Ohio River on his way back to Washington and making placid remarks about river transportation. The financial interests, however, were not so carefree. The newspapers and the radios were full of wildly optimistic stories. Professor Fisher of Yale, for example, said that stock prices were too low—and suggested that this was a good time for the smart investor to buy. Prices had to go up! In Washington Andrew Mellon, Secretary of the Treasury, assured the nation that business was basically sound. Charles E. Mitchell of the National City Bank, returned from a European trip that Monday to tell the nation that he saw nothing to be alarmed about. The market, he explained, had simply experienced a "normal shaking-out," which would prepare it for a still greater spiral of growth. Market newsletters and tip sheets, which had proliferated mightily during the past few years, all came out with the same suggestion—BUY!—and provided lists of "bargain" issues that their readers might invest in to their advantage.

The massed chorus of optimism appeared to have the desired effect. Tuesday's market staged a brisk rally. It began to sag a bit at the close, but most issues ended with net gains. Wednesday's session opened calmly. Some prices were up, and there was no shortage of buyers, but trading was rather quiet. By midmorning, however, certain auto accessory issues were battered by heavy selling. Slowly, the whole list began to slip. By 1 P.M., the decline was steep, and in the last hour a deluge of selling hit the market. The day's sales were 6,347,960 shares. *The New York Times* industrial index lost 30.97 points.

The flimsy base of the market could no longer hold. Wednesday night was a feverish one on Wall Street and in other financial centers throughout the country. Wires were humming with margin calls, and the tall buildings on the narrow streets of the financial district were lit up till the small hours of the morning. A wave of fear swept the country. Brokers, bankers, newspapers, and government officials were beseiged with phone calls. What was happening?

The next day was Thursday, October 24, 1929. Although no one had said a word, the feeling had grown that something ominous was about to happen. By ten o'clock (the hour when the stock market officially opens) every broker's office was jammed with traders. In the streets of New York's financial district crowds had gathered. No one had invited them. No announcements had been made.

People began to mass in the financial district as the feeling grew that something ominous was going to happen

No news was broadcast. But the city knew. People, many of whom had never bought a stock, massed in the narrow streets waiting expectantly—for what? When the Stock Exchange opened at ten o'clock, almost all the members were on the floor. The worst fears were realized. Enormous quantities of selling orders had accumulated overnight. During the first half-hour of trading, there were buyers to absorb them at slightly lower prices, but before the first hour was through almost all support had been exhausted. At eleven o'clock a wild stampede to sell began. Prices lurched down sharply, disastrously. There were many stocks that received no bids whatever. Floor brokers screamed and wept, they tore off their collars and coats in the struggle to keep pace with the flood of sell orders. Fear had turned to panic, and panic was dissolving into hysteria.

But the exchange, after all, is no more than an instrument—a convenient, centralized place in which to buy and sell stocks. The real panic was raging outside in the street, it swept through thousands of board rooms across the nation, it raged in banking chambers and business offices. Men trembled as they watched the terrible train of little figures that streamed from the clattering tickers. Moment by moment they watched helplessly as their hopes faded and their fortunes diminished with the descending figures on the tape.

Even more ominous, the news on the ticker tape was entirely obsolete. The ticker system had broken down completely under the volume of trading and had fallen more than an hour behind by noon. A phone call to the floor, when it could get through, reported figures that were far below those on the tape. In the absence of reliable facts, rumors swept the country. Stocks were selling for nothing, one rumor held. The Chicago and Buffalo exchanges had closed, according to another. Banks were failing by the thousands, and a suicide wave was in progress—men leaping like lemmings from skyscraper offices. The rumors persisted and grew as the market plunged.

At noon, the directors of the four greatest banks in the country met in the office of J. P. Morgan & Company, on the corner directly across from the exchange. They arrived one by one in big limousines that parked conspicuously on the crowded street. The first to arrive was Charles Mitchell of National City, then came Albert H. Wiggin of the Chase Bank, followed by William Potter and Seward Prosser of the Guaranty Trust and Banker's Trust.

They did not gather in secret as financiers generally did. They moved as conspicuously as possible. This was no financial game they were playing. The economic life of the nation was at stake. Their meeting was important psychologically as well as financially, for they were the recognized leaders of the financial community. After twenty minutes the four bankers came out and returned to their offices. Thomas Lamont, senior partner of the House of Morgan, stood on the stone steps and read this brief statement:

There has been a little distress selling on the Stock Exchange and we have held a meeting of the heads of several financial institutions to discuss the situation. We have found that there are no houses in difficulty and reports from the brokers indicate that margins are being maintained satisfactorily.

This little speech had an almost magical effect. As

soon as it had echoed through the street and penetrated to the floor of the exchange, the downward plunge of leading stocks tapered off perceptibly. A few even recovered a little.

At one o'clock, the bankers played their highest card. A bitter battle had been raging all morning to keep the stock of U.S. Steel above 200. It had opened at 205.5 but had fallen with the rest and was currently selling at 190. Steel had broken 200, a thing no one would have thought possible a few days earlier. The psychological effect of this fall was enormous.

Then Richard Whitney, vice-president of the exchange and brother to George Whitney, a partner of J. P. Morgan himself, appeared on the floor and calmly placed an order for 25,000 shares of U.S. Steel at 205, 15 points above the day's low. Then he moved around the floor placing similar orders for a score of other leading stocks. This was the support that the banking institutions offered the faltering market. For a time it worked, and prices even began to creep upward, but the gesture was too little and too late. By the end of the day everyone knew that a momentous change had occurred.

When the final bell rang, a curious sound arose from the disheveled and exhausted brokers and clerks on the floor of the exchange—a mixed chorus of boos, hoots, and catcalls. They had never made that sound before. It was spontaneous, a singular burst of disgusted sound that provided moot recognition that the golden age of Wall Street had come to an end. "Black Thursday" marked a fateful transition—an era of unrestrained business had ended in disaster. The dreams of glory and greed were over.

COLLAPSE
4

On Thursday, October 24, 1929 a panic had developed on the stock market. No one knew for certain why prices had plunged or how much further they would sink. These matters were discussed in board rooms and banks, in counting houses and executive offices across the country. It was difficult to determine what the outcome would be. During the past few years stock prices had climbed out of all proportion to reality. They were supported almost wholly by dreams of avarice and optimism —these and a flimsy credit structure. The jolt in the market had brought awareness of the reality and in the light of realism support disappeared.

Yet, the industry of America was intact. There was no earthquake, no terrible fire or natural disaster; no bombs had destroyed our industrial capacity. The factories and machines were working, farms were operating, retail stores continued doing a brisk business. Nothing fundamental had changed. Stock prices had tumbled, but confidence had also tumbled along with the stocks—and the whole structure had been held together by confidence.

The solution appeared simple: restore confidence, and everything would fall back into place. This was exactly what the financial experts and leaders attempted to do. Bankers and financial moguls; governors, mayors, Senators, Congressmen, even the President; economists and market analysts; industrialists—all joined the chorus. Beginning on Friday and continuing through that fateful weekend, newspapers and radio all over the country repeated the same message: Things were great, never better, the economy was intact and there was nothing to worry about. Variations of the same theme were repeated in newsletters and tipsheets and were even preached from pulpits at Sunday sermons.

Charles E. Mitchell of the National City Bank said, "I am of the opinion that the reaction had badly overrun itself."

M. C. Brush, president of American International, said, "I do not look for a repetition of Thursday."

Andrew Mellon, Secretary of the Treasury, said, "The economy is sound."

The message was carried from coast to coast. Bankers pledged their resources to defend the market. The full force of this propaganda barrage engulfed the country, and it seemed to work. On Friday, the optimists were quick to point out, prices had held despite heavy trading. The three-hour Saturday trading session had also been firm. The crisis was over, was the happy consensus, and the nation heaved a collective sigh of relief. But was it over?

Over that same weekend, several million investors came up with the same idea. The crisis was over, they thought, but this just might be the right time to get out while the getting was still good. Even more serious was another development. While the flood of optimistic words washed over the country, the corporations that had extended lavish sums as "call money" began to get worried. Exactly as the *Times* editor had predicted, "the unusual sources of credit" were failing the bull market. Corporations were calling back their money. The banks that regulated the flow saw the handwriting on the wall and made quiet arrangements to dispose of the securities they had bought to support the market on Thursday. The banks could no longer be depended upon to stem the selling rush— another not very promising sign.

But this was not the end. Still another serious weakness came to light as the bookkeepers and accountants tallied up the sheets for the past week's trading. Thursday's flood had swamped the brokers' clerical facilities, and they could not catch up with the paperwork until Sunday. When all the accounts were finally balanced, there was an ominous backlog of margins that had to be paid— bigger than anyone had thought possible. All Saturday and Sunday the margin calls went out. The answers were always the same: "Sell out," answered the small investor. "Sell for anything you can get. I'm through!"

On Monday, October 28, the worst fears were realized. It was a rout. The banking pool that was expected to guard price levels did not materialize. Leading stocks broke through the support levels that had been set by the banking pool as soon as trading started and kept sinking all day. Periodically rumors flashed across the floor. The banking pool was about to stem the tide; or corporation money was coming in a flood. But nothing of the sort happened. When the market finally closed, 9,212,800 shares had been traded. The *Times* index of industrials had fallen almost 50 points. Indeed, the entire list showed alarming losses. More margin calls were on their way to those speculators who had not already sold out. More calls were being sent out to recoup "call money."

In the hope of stemming the tide both U.S. Steel and American Can announced a bonus dividend. Ordinarily such an action automatically results in a rise in the stock price, but it did not happen. For all the effect the gesture had, Steel and Can might just as well have canceled their dividends entirely. Both plunged steeply along with the rest of the list.

The next day, Tuesday, October 29, was the worst. Another backlog of sell orders had accumulated overnight, and in the first half hour of trading 3,259,800 shares changed hands. The selling pressure was wholly without precedent. Nothing like this had ever happened before. It was coming from everywhere. Buyers disappeared. Often the specialists stood baffled at their posts with sellers pressing around them and not a single buyer at any price. The bottom had fallen out of the market.

This was no longer panic. It was hysteria. There was no support—not from the banks, not from the huge investment trusts, and certainly not from the small speculator. When the closing bell rang the great bull market was dead. There was no longer any doubt. Some 16,400,000 shares had changed hands, and no one will

Headlines from The New York Times *tell the story of those tense but still hopeful days in October, 1929*

ever know how many shares simply could not find buyers. Leading stocks had lost as much as 77 per cent of their peak value. So drastic was the fall, that it affected everyone. Small speculators were wiped out along with some of the biggest and most experienced traders. So violent was the crash, that the entire financial structure of the nation was shaken to its foundations. Many bankers and brokers were doubtful about their own solvency, for accounting had broken down. The truth was buried somewhere beneath a mountain of scribbled papers which would require a week of solid work to clear away.

Who was to blame? This was a question everyone asked, for the feeling was widespread that somewhere someone or something had engineered both the boom and the bust for their own nefarious end. The truth, however, was more complex than that. John Kenneth Galbraith assessed the situation more realistically than most observers when he said:

No one was responsible for the great Wall Street crash. No one engineered the speculation that preceded it. Both were the product of the free choice and decision of hundreds of thousands of individuals. The latter were not led to the slaughter. They were impelled to it by the seminal lunacy which has always seized people who are seized in turn with the notion that they can become very rich.

A dazed and shocked nation paused after this debacle to count its loss. The big question now was how and how much the crash would affect the nation's economic life. No one doubted that there would be an effect, but no one was certain what that effect might be. The phenomenon itself was completely bewildering. The country's real wealth had not been diminished by so much as a single automobile tire or one railroad engine, but its paper wealth as measured in stock prices had been cut almost in half.

Some $35,000,000,000 had vanished from the economy. Where had this wealth gone? Hundreds of thousands of peoples who had considered themselves rich now considered themselves poor. Stock certificates that only yesterday had been the keys to wealth, power, and position were suddenly pieces of printed paper without worth. No amount of cheerleading could reverse the magic and make them valuable once more.

Not that it wasn't tried. A massed chorus of business and government leaders attempted to convince the nation that the crash was not real. Everything was fine, they said, in effect. October, they pointed out, had been the all-time record month in industry after industry. The first nine months of 1929 had been better than the same period in 1928. Indeed, it had been better than any similar period in American history. Corporate earnings were at record heights, as were retail sales, exports, and manufacturing output. The *Saturday Evening Post* told the nation in full page advertisements that:

Wall Street may sell stocks, but Main Street is still buying goods.

The ticker may slow down, but production is going right ahead.

The amazing thing was that both of these statements were still somewhat true. The buying of average goods, of the day-to-day necessities, had not been affected. Production, on the other hand, though still at high levels had begun to respond to the crash. Actually, it had been sagging somewhat during the past six months. The crash merely accelerated the process. The steel industry, for example, which had been operating at 100 per cent capacity for months, had begun to slip in June and was down to 67 per cent at the end of October. Building permits were also in a decline that dipped sharply in response to the crash. In November they were down almost 65 per cent from the figure of the preceding year. Inventories of such hard goods as automobiles and appliances were overloaded and cutbacks in production were becoming frequent. The most significant of all indices, "employment in manufacturing industries, adjusted for seasonal variations," was also falling. During November it dropped 2.2 per cent which meant that during those thirty days one man in fifty had lost his job and had been unable to find another.

The most immediate effect of the crash, however, was felt in the sale of luxury goods. The demand for jewelry, as an example, plummeted with the fall in stock prices. The effects were so swift that almost all the diamond-cutting shops of Holland, which sold more than 60 per cent of their output in America, had either closed down completely or drastically cut production by November 17. Sales of limousines, furs, and penthouse apartments almost stopped. Yacht-building, which had been in the midst of a spectacular boom, came to a standstill, and boatyards all over the country were littered with half-finished yachts, their construction curtailed. Most of them were never finished. The wealthy were firing servants, and the advertisements for luxury goods that had filled the pages of slick periodicals disappeared overnight. No more dramatic index to the tenor of the times could be had than comparing an October issue of a magazine with a December issue of the same year.

It did not take long, however, for reduced demand to spread to other areas. The speculative boom had acted as a smokescreen that obscured fundamental weaknesses in the economy. Now that the smokescreen had been cleared away by the crash, these weak spots were suddenly painfully obvious. The most far-reaching problem, economists realized, was the lack of purchasing power of the great bulk of the population. Wealth had accumulated dangerously in comparatively few hands. In retrospect, this factor was obvious.

Far from being healthy, the economy of 1929 was fundamentally unsound. Throughout the twenties both production and productivity per worker expanded steadily. Between 1919 and 1929 this increase in output per worker had risen by some 43 per cent. Wages, salaries, and prices, however, remained comparatively stable. Costs fell, but prices remained the same. The result was an enormous growth of profits. It was these profits, in large part, that had gone into the booming securities speculation.

The result was a concentration of wealth in the hands of fewer people. Although the figures available are not completely accurate, it has been estimated that the 5 per cent of the population with the highest incomes in 1929 received more than one-third of all personal income. The proportion of income that came from interest, dividends and rent—the income of the rich—swelled this figure even more.

According to the best estimates, then, 5 per cent of the population had amassed as much as 40 per cent of the wealth. Such a highly unequal distribution of income meant that the economy was largely dependent on a high level of investment or a high level of luxury consumer spending or both. Since there is only so much bread that one can buy, the excess wealth must be funneled into investment or luxuries. Such spending is subject, inevitably, to more erratic influences and to wider ups and downs than the bread-and-butter outlays of the working man who earns $35 a week. This high-bracket spending and investment was especially influenced by the crushing stock market collapse.

The other source of spending support, the 60 per cent of the nation's wealth in the hands of 95 per cent of the nation's wage earners could not overcome the depressing influence of the high-bracket spending curtailments. For a time, ordinary goods continued to sell briskly, but the level began to fall precipitously. People simply did not have the money with which to buy the things they needed or wanted. Wages, as we have already seen, had not kept pace with the rest of the economy in the booming 1920s. So long as the boom lasted, this did not make very much difference. Jobs were plentiful, and, with the help of installment credit, purchasing levels remained fairly high.

The average wage earner, however, was never able to put aside any substantial reserve. On the contrary, he had mortgaged his future earnings to an amount in excess of some $15,000,000,000 in the form of installment credit. At this time, also, there was no such thing as Social Security, unemployment insurance, or even welfare programs. The worker was completely dependent upon his salary. Should his salary fail there was nothing he could fall back upon. And jobs were failing. All over the country industry was in retrenchment. At best, manufacturers were going on half-time. At worst, they were closing down completely—and the worst was more common than the best.

The cycle that had stimulated the boom reversed itself. Instead of increased demand, followed by expanded production, followed by more employment, followed by higher purchasing power and still more demand, an opposite cycle had come into effect. Less employment meant less purchasing power, which meant less demand, which meant less production, which meant less employment—a vicious cycle that was spiraling downward with no floor in sight. The elements that had supported the boom were gone. Where once everything seemed to focus on prosperity, they now pointed the way down.

And down was a nightmare. As this new cycle gained momentum, unemployment grew like a snowball rolling down a hill. In April 1930 the figure stood at 3,000,000, and within six months it had doubled. By October 1932 more than 11,000,000 people were without jobs, and by March 1933 the figure stood somewhere between 13,000,-000 and 15,000,000 and was probably higher because it did not count the youth who had never worked and who now competed for a dwindling number of jobs.

The effects of the depression were very different for the wealthy as compared with the poor. The wealthy may have had to give up a yacht, or close down their Newport beach cottage, and most had to cut down on their servant staffs. For the wage earner who had depended completely upon his salary, the effects were catastrophic. What little savings he might have had were either exhausted or even lost in a bank failure. Without a job, he had nothing. There was no money with which to buy food, no money with which to pay the rent, no money with which to buy clothes.

Overnight millions became destitute. Unemployed men and women tried to sell apples on street corners. Mortgages were foreclosed, and the owners lost their homes. Those who rented apartments were evicted when they could not pay the rent. Some people starved to death. Others lived in shacks and hovels put together out of the

(*Above*) *Soup kitchens and bread lines became a familiar sight in America; (right) mortgages were foreclosed and people were evicted from their homes*

refuse of the cities. Hundreds of thousands of young people left their homes and wandered around the country, riding in freight cars or begging rides on the highways. Many had left their homes because their families could no longer feed them. Rather than remain and see younger brothers and sisters suffer, they left to make out as best they could. At least their departure would mean fewer hungry mouths for their families to feed.

Many millions were forced to turn to public charity in order to exist. But then in 1931 even the relief system broke down. Entire municipalities were bankrupt. They could no longer pay the salaries of teachers and policemen, let alone finance relief for destitute families. Breadlines and soup kitchens where long queues of people lined up for a bowl of soup or a slice of bread—often the only thing that stood between them and starvation—became a familiar sight in all American cities.

Many people lived in shacks—some of them
in the shadow of luxury apartment buildings
along Central Park

Between the years 1929 and 1933 the gross national product of the United States—the total of goods and services produced—had fallen by almost half. As a statistic this figure can hardly begin to describe the suffering that it represented. It meant the difference between hope and despair; between a roof over your head and homeless, vagrant existence; between clothes on your back and rags; between an adequate income and poverty.

Overnight a prosperous and confident nation had descended into poverty and despair. And things kept getting worse rather than better, reaching the lowest point in 1933. In the midst of this decline, the industrial capacity of America sat idle. Everything necessary for prosperity was available, the machinery as well as the know-how, technical prowess, and organizational abilities. Never had America experienced such a contradiction. People were out of work, but the machines were idle. People needed clothes, houses, automobiles, but the factories and builders did nothing. People were starving, but crops had not been sown or were rotting unharvested in the fields.

This was the greatest tragedy of all. The machinery for prosperity was here, but the prime moving force was no longer in operation. The depression was not caused by any natural failure. There was no shortage of either the raw materials or the means by which they are transformed into useful products. It was the failure of a system in which the prime moving force was not the needs of the people but the ability to make a profit. Business, unrestrained by government, had demonstrated its failure to satisfy the needs of the people. It was time for a "New Deal."

FIGHTING
BACK:
TOO LITTLE
TOO LATE
5

If any factor can be singled out as the principal cause for the 1929 collapse, it must be psychological in nature. It is rooted in the tenuous, shifting moods of the public. Speculation on a large scale cannot occur without an underlying sense of confidence and optimism. There must also be faith in the good intentions and even in the benevolence of others. For people get rich, without exception, through the efforts of others. In the late twenties both the confidence and the optimism were present in abundance.

In 1929 Professor Charles Amos Dice of Ohio State University observed in an untimely book titled *New Levels in the Stock Market,* published just before the crash:

The common folks believe in their leaders. We no longer look upon the captains of industry as magnified crooks. Have we not heard their voices over the radio? Are we not familiar with their thoughts, ambitions, and ideals as they have been expressed to us almost as a man talks to his friend?

If it all sounds a bit too cosy and folksy, it is not an exaggeration. Professor Dice reflected an attitude that was common before the crash. The big financiers, the big manipulators, the big industrialists were heroes. The public looked up to them, read about them, and tried to emulate them. Their wisdom was considered beyond that of mortal man, and their fundamental benevolence was not questioned. This was the attitude of the public toward those they believed were leading the business affairs of the nation—and the business of the nation was business.

Such a feeling of trust is essential for a boom. When people are cautious, or suspicious, or prone to ask questions they are not subject to speculative enthusiasms. Booms, in historical perspective, occur generally only after long periods of prosperity, when people are confident about their future and have enough savings to risk it in the hope of gaining even more. All of these elements were present in the latter half of the twenties, and they gathered force for the speculative boom and bust that followed.

The stock market crash can be much more easily explained than the depression that followed in its wake. In retrospect, we see that there really was no good reason for the severity or extent of the economic crash. In 1929 the labor force was not tired, it could have continued producing indefinitely at the best 1929 rate. The capital plant of the country was neither depleted nor worn out.

It had been renewed and improved in the preceding years of prosperity. Entrepreneurs were never more imaginative or aggressive. Obviously if men, materials, plants and management were all there to assure continued and even enlarged production, there was no physical reason for any cutback.

Nor, as many economists of the time suggested, had the high production of the twenties outrun the needs of the people. During this period people were being supplied with an increasing volume of goods. But there is no evidence that their desire for automobiles, housing, clothing, recreation, or even food had been sated. All subsequent studies showed a capacity for a large further increase in consumption. A depression was certainly not needed to allow people's wants to catch up with their capacity to produce. Even at the height of prosperity there were more than enough poor people available to absorb all that the country could produce if they had had enough money to buy.

No, the depression was not caused by a failure in the nation's industrial capacity. It was a psychological failure that can be understood only in terms of the changing mood of the population and the vagaries of an unrestrained and unregulated capitalist economy. After the catastrophe struck, it was this psychological attitude again that made the crisis so severe and so long.

This psychological outlook, perhaps, was the most tragic feature of the depression. Some people were hungry, and some people were starving in 1930, 1931, 1932, and 1933. Others were tortured by the fear that they might go hungry also. Yet others suffered the agony of falling from the honor and respectability that goes with income into the humiliation of poverty. Still others feared that they would be next. Everyone, it seemed, suffered from a sense of complete hopelessness. A plague had been visited upon the land, and nothing could be done. This was the attitude that aggravated all problems and prevented any constructive steps for so long.

One of the factors that encouraged this defeatist attitude was the almost total absence of leadership. The nation woke up one morning to discover to its horror that "no one was minding the store." Not business and not the government. Administration policies of the past ten years had been dominated by two basic principles: noninterference in the economic affairs of the nation and a balanced budget.

The balanced budget part was understandable enough. It made sense. The government, like any respectable business or household, tried to keep its spending in line with its income. It was the first attitude, however, that was at the root of the subsequent problems. The policy of noninterference left a vacuum in a particularly vulnerable area.

Most people, quite naturally, assumed that someone was in charge although they were not certain exactly who it was. Wall Street ran things and in the popular imagination this may have been a cabal of financiers and industrialists who pulled secret strings. They were devilishly clever, fabulously wealthy, and benevolent—an enlightened plutocracy, perhaps, who looked after the welfare of the country. But then this mask of omniscience with which the public imagination had clothed the business leaders was snatched away. After the crash, the Mitchells, the Insulls, the Lamonts, the Whitneys, the

Goldmans were revealed for what they really were: human beings with all of the weakness and fallibility of mere mortals.

In reality, no one was in charge. There was no mysterious cabal, no omnipotent "Wall Street." Business was run then, as it is now, on an individual corporation basis. The leaders of both finance and industry were responsible, ultimately, only for the well-being of the organizations with which they were associated. They had to be. This is the nature of business in a free-enterprise economy. There was no single enterprise, no trust or holding company, however large and powerful, that could ignore this fact. Business was operated and maintained through the individual decisions of thousands of independent companies and corporations.

There was no central organization to coordinate this activity, and this was the problem. In the absence of centralized control, the most daring, imaginative, and *the most reckless* entrepreneurs are those who must invariably come out ahead. More important, the more conservative concerns, even those with a sense of social responsibility, are compelled into the same cycle in order to remain competitive. The manager who must make a decision in which the good of his company is opposed to the good of the public is forced to align himself on the side of the company. If he does not, his company will fall prey to those who would not hesitate in such a situation. The businessman, no matter how idealistic he may personally be, cannot afford to exercise his social conscience in the management of his business.

To illustrate this economic fact, let us imagine a situation that confronted many businessmen in the 1930s. The most pressing problem of the time was unemployment and the resulting lack of purchasing power. A responsible entrepreneur, aware of this fact, may have tried to maintain the wage scale and number of his employees, but he could do this only as long as his competitors did the same. Should one of them cut the wages or reduce the number of his employees, he would thereby gain a competitive advantage, other things being equal. The responsible employer would be compelled to follow suit or be driven out of business. Should the responsible employer persist in his idealism, the situation was such he would actually aggravate conditions. Half a work force earning reduced wages was still better than no work force at all.

The only organization with sufficient potential power to regulate business, to protect the responsible entrepreneur from his irresponsible competitors, is the federal government. In the 1920s the federal government had abdicated this responsibility. There was, consequently, no leadership and no authority that was in a position to regulate the commercial life of the country.

Nor did there appear to be any pressing need for such an authority—at least not until after the crash. So long as the economy was booming and most people were working no one complained. It seemed that unrestrained capitalism had provided the means by which the entire population could enjoy the fruits of prosperity. Most people, except for a scattered handful of Bolsheviks and wild-eyed anarchists, believed that a policy of enlightened selfishness was best.

Government concurred in this opinion and kept meddling fingers out of business affairs. Unfortunately when the crash occurred the government was not prepared either philosophically or politically to undertake any meaningful action. Outside of issuing optimistic statements, the government did nothing. As the stock market collapsed and its effects spread through the economy, President Hoover and Secretary of the Treasury Mellon were repeatedly quoted as saying, "The economy is sound. There is nothing fundamentally wrong."

Something was, of course, fundamentally wrong. The economy of the country had collapsed. Despite the cheery optimism of official pronouncements, things kept sinking. The collapse spread from the stock market to the commodities exchange where the prices of wheat, cotton, oil, iron, and copper plunged with equal drama. When the publicized "fundamentals"—freight-car loadings, pig iron and steel output, automobile and hard goods production, coal output—followed suit, even the government had to take notice.

President Hoover's first concrete step was typical. He announced a tax cut in late November 1929 the principal beneficiaries of which were large corporations and the wealthy. During a period of rising unemployment, the act was sarcastically described as "rich relief." Not only did the gesture not help the unemployed, but its effects upon the economy had no measurable influence.

Obviously something more had to be done, and President Hoover did not hesitate. He called conferences—of industrialists, economists, financiers, bankers, railroad executives, the heads of large utilities, directors of important construction firms, representatives of farm organizations, and even union leaders.

Throughout the months of November and December a steady stream of leaders came to meet with the President. The procedure in each conference was the same. First there was a solemn session with the President, then those attending had their pictures taken with him. Finally, there was a press conference during which more pictures were taken and the conferees volunteered their opinions on the problems they had discussed. These opinions, without exception, were always most favorable.

After one such meeting of industrial leaders on November 21, attended by Henry Ford, Walter Teagle, Owen D. Young, Alfred P. Sloan, Jr., Pierre duPont, Walter Gifford, and Andrew Mellon, the pronouncements were even more optimistic than usual. In fact, the expressions of confidence and optimism were so insistent and robust that Julius Rosenwald, who also attended the meeting, said that he feared that there might soon be a severe labor shortage.

Utility, banking, railroad, and construction executives were in agreement. After their conferences with the President, they were equally hopeful and optimistic. Even the leaders of farm organizations and labor unions, a notoriously pessimistic bunch, spoke optimistically. They told assembled reporters after their meeting with the President that the "morale of their members was better than it had been for years." The economists and college professors were, if anything, even more hopeful. After their conference with the President, they proved with the aid of a dazzling display of charts, figures, esoteric formulas, industrial indices, theoretical limits, and other scholarly paraphernalia that "the corner had been turned." By the end of November, they all agreed, the worst would be over and from there on in the road would be up!

This action on the part of President Hoover was hailed in the press. A Wall Street financial writer began his story of one of these sessions by writing, " 'Order up the Moors' was Marshal Foch's reply at the first battle of the Marne . . . 'Order up the business reserves,' directed President Hoover." The *Philadelphia Record* described the President as "easily the most commanding figure in the modern science of 'engineering statesmanship.' " The *Boston Globe* ecstatically told the nation that "it has at the White House a man who believes not in the philosophy of drift, but in the dynamics of mastery."

There was only one thing wrong. Despite all the reassurance, despite all the dynamic conferences things kept on going from bad to worse. As the conferences continued and nothing tangible was done, President Hoover changed rapidly from the hero of the nation to its scapegoat. His name became synonymous with depression. The shantytowns constructed on the outskirts of cities and towns by people who had lost their homes were called "Hoovervilles"; newspapers were called "Hoover blankets"; the thin soup distributed at emergency kitchens became "Hoover stew"; the fruit peddled by the unemployed on the nation's streets was called "Hoover apples"; the cardboard with which people patched the worn soles of their shoes was called "Hoover leather." Overnight, the hero became the villain.

It was not that he did not try. During the months of November and December of 1929 there were more conferences in the White House than there had been in the preceding ten years. In December he told Congress that the steps he had taken—the rich relief tax cut and the conferences—had "re-established confidence." In

March 1930 President Hoover told Congress that "the worst effects of the crash upon unemployment would be ended in sixty days." In May he said he was convinced "we have now passed the worst and with continued unity and effort shall rapidly recover." In June he said "business will be normal by fall."

He was wrong. At the time, the nation was entering the first stages of a prolonged and severe depression. All the indices kept slipping; foreign trade fell off sharply; more factories closed; banks continued to fail; company after company cancelled dividends; the number of unemployed grew alarmingly; the prices of wheat, cotton, oil, copper, and other commodities kept sinking; and now the federal surplus was turned into a deficit as government income fell. The buying power of the nation was paralyzed.

In the autumn of 1929 the bottom had fallen out of the stock market, but prices kept right on sinking. On November 13, 1929 the *Times* index of industrial averages had closed at a disastrous 224. By July 8, 1932 it had sunk to 58. Standard Oil of New Jersey, which the Rockefellers were supposed to have pegged at 50 on November 13, 1929, dropped to 18 on April 15, 1932. U. S. Steel, which sold in September 1929 for 262, was going begging at 22 in 1932. Montgomery Ward was 4, down from 138. The big trusts were battered even more. The prices of stock in such once spectacular trusts as Blue Ridge and Shenandoah, which had sold for more than $100, were quoted at 50 and 75 cents, respectively, in 1932.

More dramatic was the decline in the nation's production levels. During the week of July 8, 1932, iron and steel production had sunk to some 12 per cent of capacity. Pig iron output was the lowest since the panic year of

1896. That same week the *Commercial and Financial Chronicle* observed that "copper shares are so low that their fluctuations are of little consequence."

The nation sought desperately for leadership, but the Republican administration could not provide it at the necessary level. It was psychologically and philosophically incapable of taking the drastic action needed to make the economy move. The attitude of noninterference that had served the Republicans so well in the past now compounded an already grave situation.

In response to overwhelming public pressure, President Hoover appointed a cabinet committee in October 1930 to formulate measures for the relief of unemployment. That December he laid before Congress a program for road construction, public buildings, flood control, and airways development projects to employ idle workers. He also signed twenty-two bills appropriating $300,000,000 for loans to farmers, drought relief, and emergency construction. That month he also organized a voluntary $500,000,000 bankers pool to help rescue the weaker banks from failure. None of the measures worked. The appropriations were too small to prime the economy and the bankers pool, being basically voluntary in nature soon disintegrated.

Again, Hoover's measures had no appreciable effect. More stringent action was called for to confront the emergency. On January 22, 1932 President Hoover signed the bill creating the $2,000,000,000 Reconstruction Finance Corporation (R.F.C.), which was empowered to make funds available to banks, insurance companies, agricultural associations and railroads, and to those states that needed financial assistance. This act, the most sweeping of his

*All through 1930 banks
continued to fail as
people demanded their
savings*

administration, would, the President hoped, start the wheels of industry rolling once more.

As it turned out, the R.F.C. was not broad enough to have more than limited results. The appropriations helped save some banks and prevented the bankruptcy of a few railroads. It provided salaries for unpaid teachers, police, and firemen in many municipalities; it also made loans that began the construction of New York State's Jones Beach, San Francisco's Oakland Bay Bridge, the Pennsylvania Turnpike, and other worthwhile projects. As the first program for federal aid, it established a precedent for the hundreds of agencies and public works projects which were to come later under a new administration.

As a prime moving force in the economy, however, the R.F.C. failed. Despite its broad scope, it could not provide enough purchasing power to revitalize industry. Most significant, the measure did not stop the growth of unemployment. Economic conditions kept worsening. More banks failed, more businesses closed, many cities were bankrupt, the relief system had long since broken down and more than a third of the labor force was without work. For millions of Americans life had become a nightmare of despair.

One of the final acts of the Hoover administration marked the complete bankruptcy of the Republican philosophy of "business comes first." During the summer of 1932 thousands of unemployed veterans converged upon Washington, D.C. They came from all over the nation in a spontaneous and ill-organized march. In

Thousands of unemployed veterans converged on Washington demanding a bonus, jobs and relief

General Douglas MacArthur (left) with his junior officer Major Dwight D. Eisenhower (right). Under MacArthur's orders the army drove out the veterans and burned their shacks (opposite)

the capital, they demanded a veteran's bonus, jobs, and relief for the poor and starving in America. They vowed that they would stay until their demands were met. For two months the veterans' army besieged the capital. Most lived in a shantytown—a "Hooverville"—constructed just outside the city on Anacostia flats, but some simply set up housekeeping on the grass in front of public monuments. Neither Congress nor the President were inclined to act on their demands.

Instead the veterans were driven from the city. On the afternoon of July 28, 1932 Secretary of War Patrick J. Hurley, acting under direct instructions from the White House, ordered General Douglas MacArthur, Chief of the United States Army, to "surround the affected areas and clear them without delay."

At 4:30 P.M., General MacArthur issued his orders. Troops led by cavalry and followed by tanks, machine gunners, and infantry rumbled down Pennsylvania Avenue driving the veterans before them. Tear gas quickly routed those who sought refuge in buildings. The bonus marchers were driven across the bridge to the "Hooverville" they had set up at Anacostia. The troops did not stop here. More tear gas cleared the area and fire bombs finished the operation. The shacks were engulfed in flames and smoke. They burned to the ground within hours.

All that night and the next day pathetic groups of men could be seen straggling along the roads leading from the capital. They were like a defeated army, without bravado or spirit. Disorganized and weaponless, they could not stand up to the well-equipped legions of General MacArthur.

The bonus march was defeated and the capital was safe from its own veterans. The Hoover administration had won the battle, but it had lost the war. When American soldiers were called upon to march against American veterans in the country's capital, it marked the last gasp of a thoroughly discredited policy. Three months later, President Hoover and his administration were to suffer the most telling defeat of any presidential candidate in American political history.

"HAPPY DAYS ARE HERE AGAIN"

6

When Hoover took office on March 4, 1929 the nation was at a peak of prosperity. When he relinquished office four years later, the country was in crisis. Much of the onus for this catastrophe was put on President Hoover. His reserves of public support, respect, and affection plummeted in proportion to the growth of unemployment and the spread of poverty. His name became a byword for depression. Yet despite all the "Hoovervilles," despite the fiasco of the veterans' march, Hoover was renominated by the Republican Party as their presidential candidate on the first ballot at the 1932 party convention in Chicago.

Republican Party leaders had no choice. To repudiate President Hoover, even in the face of his dwindling public support and respect, would have been a repudiation of twelve years of Republican policy. It would have been tantamount to an admission that the political philosophy upon which Republican policy had been based was a mistake. Like it or not, the party was stuck with its leader. The party platform could offer nothing better than more of the same. In his acceptance speech at the convention, President Hoover reiterated his belief that "the economy was basically sound."

Hoover's Democratic opponent, nominated in the same Chicago convention hall a few weeks later, was Franklin Delano Roosevelt, governor of New York State. The outcome of the presidential election was never seriously in doubt. Roosevelt expected to win, and most political observers agreed that he would. Hoover and his Republican administration had been thoroughly discredited. All their attempts to revive the economy had come to nothing.

The country was crying for change. And change—a New Deal!—was what a vigorous Democratic candidate promised a stricken nation, change that would irrevocably alter the relation between business and government.

Considering his background and education, Franklin Delano Roosevelt was a most unlikely candidate for popular reform. He was not born in a log cabin, nor even in a prairie town like Herbert Hoover. He was born on a comfortable estate in Hyde Park, New York, on January 30, 1882 to a patrician family that traced its ancestry to the earliest Dutch settlers of the New World. There was little in his early years to suggest the dramatic turn his life was destined to take.

Franklin Delano Roosevelt was the only son of James and Sara Delano Roosevelt. His father, well into his fifties at the time of Franklin's birth, was a gentleman farmer and a Democrat, unexpectedly, who had interests in railroads and coal lands and was for some years vice-president of the Delaware and Hudson Railroad. Sara Delano Roosevelt, only half her husband's age, came from a wealthy family of New York and New England merchants and coal magnates.

Although the total wealth of the family was modest when compared to some of the huge fortunes of the day, it placed the Roosevelts in the millionaire category. More important, it was old established wealth that included unassailable social position. The family lived in unostentatious luxury, dividing the year between the Hyde Park estate and European social centers. From the time he was three years old, young Franklin was taken abroad for part of almost every year.

Until the age of fourteen he was tutored privately at home and learned French and German along with his other academic studies. It was a pattern of living enjoyed by a small, tightly knit circle of established wealth and social position. Franklin was raised in this tradition. He was expected to be a gentleman, trained to maintain his social position and standing, and taught to exercise an attitude of responsibility towards those less fortunate.

When Franklin was 14, and a rather shy youth, according to contemporary reports, he was enrolled at the Groton school. Groton was modeled after the public schools of England. Its student body was exclusive, limited to representatives of those families who combined wealth and position. The director of the school, Rector Endicott Peabody, trained rich young men here to exercise responsible stewardship through public service.

*Franklin D. Roosevelt and his mother Sara, at Hyde Park, the
year before he went to Groton*

At Groton Franklin did not make many friends, nor did he distinguish himself academically or in sports—upon which Groton placed strong emphasis.

After graduating from Groton, the next step in the education of the young man of Franklin's class was Harvard. Here, he lost much of his early shyness and became more active socially, participating in numerous extracurricular activities. In his senior year, he was chief editor of the school newspaper, *The Harvard Crimson*.

Still an undistinguished scholar, he was, nevertheless, exposed to the broad liberal education that Harvard afforded its students. In the field of economics, he was influenced by the liberal school that advocated progressive governmental regulation of economic affairs. His linguistic abilities were also sharpened, and young Franklin was fluent in French and German when he graduated. His trilingual ability was to serve him well in the future.

The most important political influence of his college years, however, was provided by his glamorous distant relative, Theodore Roosevelt, a fifth cousin, who was President of the United States and a champion of progressive reform. Franklin voted for him in the 1904 election and campaigned actively on his behalf among his fellow students before his graduation that year. This experience gave young Roosevelt his first taste of politics— a taste that was to dominate the rest of his life.

Besides actively campaigning for President Theodore Roosevelt in his senior year at Harvard, Franklin also met the President's niece, Eleanor Roosevelt. Outwardly, the two appeared to have little in common outside of background and social position. By this time, Franklin had changed from a shy youth into an active, outgoing, and

AFTER THE CRASH   102

vigorous young man. Eleanor, quiet and rather plain, was painfully shy. She was a social worker active in settlement work in New York City. Her work brought her into close contact with the city's poor and her sympathetic concern opened Franklin's eyes to the terrible conditions of the underprivileged in New York slums. They were married on March 17, 1905.

After graduating from Harvard, Franklin enrolled at the Columbia University Law School and was admitted to the bar in 1908. He did not, however, complete the necessary courses for an Ll.B. degree. After being admitted to the bar, Franklin worked as a clerk for the Wall Street law firm of Carter, Ledyard, and Milburn for several years. Actually his interest in law had already become a secondary concern, for he had decided upon a career in public service. His admiration for Theodore Roosevelt, who urged young men of substance to enter public service, together with the promptings of his wife and his own preference, led him to politics.

His first political opportunity came in 1910 when the Democratic Party leaders of Dutchess County, New York, persuaded him to undertake a campaign for the state senate. The nomination was considered no more than a formality, since no one expected the Democratic candidate to defeat the Republican incumbent for the office. Roosevelt, not yet twenty-nine years old at the time, surprised everyone by winning the seat in a stunning upset. He campaigned vigorously and imaginatively throughout Dutchess County, displaying a natural political acumen and an ability to win votes. He was elected to office by a substantial majority.

As a state senator, Franklin gained a reputation as an

Franklin D. Roosevelt and Eleanor Roosevelt at the time of their engagement in 1903

independent who stood up successfully against the big city political machines which dominated the political life of the state. Within a few days after taking his seat, he won state and even national acclaim by leading a group of Democratic insurgents opposed to the nominee for United States Senator that was sponsored by Tammany Hall, the New York City Democratic organization. For three months Franklin held the insurgents together until Tammany Hall finally capitulated and switched to another candidate. In this affair Franklin acted as a conservative, "clean-government" Democrat, but he had earned the "insurgent" label which made him increasingly popular among rural and upstate agricultural factions.

His two years in the state senate brought Franklin into contact with most of the important New York political figures. A political novice when he took office, he learned quickly and was soon looked upon as a shrewd bargainer with a sure political instinct. His political techniques and philosophy were influenced by such Democratic leaders as James Walker, later mayor of New York City, Alfred E. Smith, and Robert F. Wagner, Sr. As he learned and mastered the political arts under their tutelage, Roosevelt gradually abandoned the patrician airs and attitudes he had brought to the state senate.

An active supporter of Woodrow Wilson in his campaign for the presidency, Roosevelt was rewarded with an appointment as assistant secretary of the navy on March 13, 1913. Here, the young man from New York demonstrated remarkable administrative abilities. In this office Roosevelt gained valuable experience in the intricacies of governmental procedures on the federal level. During the war years, he distinguished himself as a sympathetic and skillful negotiator with the labor unions among the civilian employees in naval shipyards.

At the Democratic convention in 1920 Roosevelt was nominated for the office of vice-president. Although he campaigned vigorously with James M. Cox, the presidential nominee, the Democratic candidates were defeated in the Republican landslide. Without public office for the first time in ten years, Franklin Roosevelt turned temporarily to private life. He took a position with the Fidelity and Deposit Company of Maryland, a bonding company, and, like so many of his contemporaries during the boom years of the 1920s, entered into numerous business ventures, many of a speculative nature.

He remained active in politics during this period as an advisor and consultant in the New York State Democratic Party organization. Then came one of those tragedies that can strike anyone, rich or poor. In August 1921, while vacationing with his family at Campobello Island, New Brunswick, Roosevelt was stricken with poliomyelitis. Thirty-nine years old at the time, at the height of his physical maturity, he was almost completely paralyzed by the dread disease. He suffered intensely but refused to give way to depression. Instead, he fought back. He concentrated all of his energies upon rehabilitation and predicted gaily that he would soon regain the use of his legs.

His doctors, however, were more pessimistic. Franklin Roosevelt would never be able to walk again without assistance. His mother urged him to retire from public life and live at the family estate in Hyde Park. Franklin, however, never seriously considered retirement. Eleanor Roosevelt, his wife, and Louis Howe, his secretary, also urged him to continue. Both felt that he could still contribute importantly to the political life of the nation and that continued activity was necessary for his morale and mental well-being.

Within two weeks after Roosevelt was stricken, while still bedridden and almost completely paralyzed, he was dictating political letters. Though he was unable to attend public gatherings and meetings, Mrs. Roosevelt and Howe attended for him. Although naturally shy and retiring, Mrs. Roosevelt overcame her shyness through the forces of circumstance and the skilled tutelage of Louis Howe and became an effective political worker and public speaker.

Bedridden and unable to run for office, Roosevelt nevertheless continued functioning effectively as a premature "elder statesman" to the party. Most of his political activity during this period of Republican domination was centered on promoting unity among the urban and rural wings of the Democratic Party. Himself a rural Democrat, Roosevelt nominated Governor Alfred E. Smith of New York, the favorite of the big city factions, at the 1924 and 1928 conventions.

When Smith won the Democratic nomination for president in 1928, he urged Roosevelt to run for his vacated office of governor. Roosevelt hesitated for a number of reasons. He could not walk without braces and assistance. The doctors had been right. Although Roosevelt had worked constantly since 1921 to try to regain the use of his legs, his efforts had been in vain. He had consulted many doctors and had undergone numerous courses of treatment. Beginning in 1924 he had spent part of each year at Warm Springs, Georgia, where the naturally hot, mineralized waters combined with a systematic program of therapy brought substantial improvement in his condition. Indeed, except for the use of his legs, Roosevelt had regained his health and the buoyant optimism that had always been a part of him.

In the year 1928 a Democratic candidate for any office could expect strong opposition. The nation was dominated by a Republican administration that had brought an unprecedented wave of prosperity. Throughout the country, Republican candidates for public offices reflected and shared the respect commanded by their party. The political pickings for Democrats were slim.

Nevertheless, Roosevelt accepted the nomination and ran for the office of governor of New York. It was a gamble. A defeat, which appeared to be almost certain, could very well have meant the end of his political career. Accepting the challenge, Roosevelt threw himself into the campaign with characteristic vigor. He traveled all over the state by automobile and train. Despite the fact that he could not walk, Roosevelt demonstrated all of the youthful zest and buoyancy that had always made him so attractive a political candidate.

In the campaign he also revealed another side of his personality. The years of struggle to recover from the ravages of polio had made subtle changes. Roosevelt emerged as a more mature, more humane candidate. He had lost the use of his legs but had grown in stature as a human being, and he was somehow able to project this quality to the public.

As he expected, his opponents raised the question of his

After his election as governor of New York, Roosevelt gradually came to realize that government must play a larger role in regulating business

health as a campaign issue. Roosevelt answered these charges by conducting a vigorous campaign. He traveled widely throughout the state and spoke before so many people that his activity effectively disposed of the health issue. In the national elections Smith was defeated in the Hoover landslide and failed to carry New York State. Roosevelt, in another stunning political upset, was elected with a plurality of 25,000 votes. At that time the governor's term of office in New York State was two years.

Before he became governor, Franklin Roosevelt's policies and political outlooks were not much further left than those of President Hoover. He had been, basically, a conservative who advocated clean government with a minimum of interference in the business affairs of the state. After his election as governor, however, his outlook changed, and he gradually came to the realization that government must play a larger role.

One of his first acts as governor, for example, was the passage of a tax relief program for the benefit of the small farmers in New York who were finding it increasingly difficult to maintain their holdings. He also came into open battle with the public utilities over rate structures. Roosevelt felt that since the utilities were legitimatized monopolies, the rates they charged consumers should be regulated by municipal and state authorities.

As governor, Roosevelt also forced a bill through the state legislature authorizing the initial steps toward the development of the enormous resources of the St. Lawrence River. His plan included not only a state-owned and supervised electrical generating capacity, but also the opening of the Great Lakes to ocean shipping through a series of canals and a dredged deepwater channel through the river. These programs alienated him from the regular Democratic Party apparatus of the state, but they earned him the respect of the voters. This, coupled with the deepening economic crisis, led to Roosevelt's reelection in 1930 with an overwhelming plurality of 750,000 votes.

During this second administration Roosevelt's basic political policy moved steadily to the left. Where he had been a conservative, he was now becoming a radical. Depression had gripped the nation, and Roosevelt was able to witness at first hand the suffering and privation that the economic collapse brought in its wake. He acted to mobilize the machinery of the state government to aid the economy and to alleviate the conditions of the poor and unemployed. Toward this end, Roosevelt obtained legislation establishing the Temporary Emergency Relief Administration, the first of the country's state relief agencies, and began a broad program of state-supported public works to relieve the plight of the unemployed.

This new thrust of policy, which had been demanded by economic conditions, brought the governor into direct opposition with the conservative elements in the state legislature. In his battles for meaningful social legislation, Roosevelt sharpened the skills of political maneuver and persuasion that would be vital were he to become President. No one doubted that this was the office upon which Franklin Roosevelt had set his sights. After his decisive victory in 1930, he emerged as his party's foremost figure and leading presidential aspirant.

There was, however, a serious problem that had to be overcome. It took a two-thirds vote for a candidate to win the nomination. Although Roosevelt had rallied considerable national support, he had also generated opposition. His aggressive formulation of radical bills in the state legislature alienated many party leaders. Alfred Smith, for example, who had previously been an ally now openly led the opposition.

In order to consolidate his support, Roosevelt began a systematic campaign. Louis Howe, his secretary, conducted an intensive letter-writing campaign and James A. Farley, a leader in the New York State Democratic apparatus who had allied himself with Roosevelt, conducted skillful negotiations with Democratic leaders throughout the country. Roosevelt's principal strength, it was apparent, was among the progressive and intellectual factions of the party. He also had a strong following in the agricultural areas of the south and west and in rural areas generally. His strongest opposition came from urban and conservative eastern Democrats who were still loyal to Al Smith.

Roosevelt came to the 1932 convention with a majority of the delegates committed to him, but did not have enough votes for the two-thirds majority necessary for nomination. His opponents, though not strong enough to win the nomination, were in a position to prevent his winning the nomination. For a time, it looked as though the convention would be locked. Then, on the third ballot, John Nance Garner, the Texas favorite son candidate who had also won the California primary, released his delegates to vote for Roosevelt. The deadlock was broken. Roosevelt was nominated for the presidency with Garner as his vice-presidential running mate.

There was only one issue in the 1932 presidential election—the depression. Prohibition, which had split the Democratic party into the "wet" urban and "dry" rural factions through the 1920s, was no longer vital; the platform pledged repeal. In a well-organized and -directed effort, Roosevelt campaigned with characteristic vigor and energy. Displaying smiling confidence and verve, he traveled across the country by train, automobile, and airplane, outlining a program for recovery and reform that he called the "New Deal." The theme song of the campaign was "Happy Days Are Here Again," and its catchy tune was soon being sung by the whole country.

In a series of speeches and radio talks prepared by a team of writers, which included playwright Sherwood Anderson, Roosevelt presented his program to the people. He promised aid to farmers, public development of electric power, a balanced budget, vastly expanded public works projects, and relief programs for the unemployed. Outlined in these speeches was a program that would drastically alter the traditional role of government. Roosevelt called for an end to the laissez-faire attitude that gave business a free and unrestrained hand. He called for federal regulation of utilities and the operation of the stock market.

It was a program that appealed to millions who had been Republicans and millions who were frightened and bewildered over the collapse of the American economy. President Hoover, campaigning for reelection, termed Roosevelt's program "socialistic" and outlined his own plan for remedying the depression. He could not, however, overcome the onus of the "Hoovervilles," the growing unemployment, and the dismal failure of the veterans' march.

Many observers felt that Hoover's personal unpopularity, rather than Roosevelt's persuasiveness, was the principal cause of the one-sided Democratic victory in November 1932. Roosevelt came to office in a Democratic landslide, receiving 22,821,857 votes to Hoover's 15,761,-841. The electoral vote was 472 to 59, and the Democrats also won substantial majorities in both houses of Congress. The results were clear and unquestionable. The people of America had given Franklin Delano Roosevelt a decisive mandate. It was time for change, and he was to be the instrument of that change.

WASHINGTON
ALPHABET SOUP
7

Franklin Delano Roosevelt was elected, and Herbert
Clark Hoover was defeated. A new party, a new administration, and a new policy had won the day. Yet there was
and still is a tendency to exaggerate the differences between the two men and their policies. In actual fact, the
programs advocated by the two candidates in that fateful
election were not so terribly different. Some two years
after the election, Walter Lippmann was able to write in
his syndicated column in an article assessing President
Roosevelt's program that "most of President Roosevelt's
recovery program is an evolution from President Hoover's." It was a statement that was popular with neither
Democrats or Republicans. The Republicans were determined to view the New Deal as a wicked descent into

"socialism," while the Democrats were zealous in their claim to beneficent originality.

Lippmann's observation, however, was apt and to the point. Both presidents acted within the framework of the American constitution and the economic system that evolved under the peculiar conditions of the American experience. Within the limits of this capitalistic, free-enterprise system, there was only so much that the government could do to alleviate the crisis. Both leaders took unprecedented action to attempt to bring the country's economic mechanism back into working order. In both cases the principal method was that of "pump-priming"— creating jobs and increasing purchasing power through public works, spreading the available work in the private sectors of the economy by encouraging shorter work hours, raising farm prices through governmental support programs, expanding credit through the Federal Reserve System.

Hoover's Reconstruction Finance Corporation and Home Loan Banks, for example, continued under the Democratic administration throughout the period of crisis. What Roosevelt did, basically, was to introduce more of the same on a broader scale. The most significant difference between the two candidates was psychological rather than philosophical or political. Neither was a revolutionary. There was, however, a world of difference between Hoover's cautious reluctance in adopting these measures and Roosevelt's unabashed zest for experiment and innovation. Where Hoover hesitated, Roosevelt plunged ahead and invited the nation to follow.

It was this quality of Roosevelt's that turned the tables on the Republican's most widely used tactic. Roosevelt's opponents never tired of pointing out that Roosevelt was born with a silver spoon in his mouth, that he had the traditional aristocratic disdain for money. Hoover, on the other hand, was a self-made farm boy from Iowa who worked his way through school by taking in laundry and who knew the value of a dollar. As private citizen and as governor of New York, Roosevelt was an easy spender. More important, he was unimpressed by the financiers and industrialists of Wall Street and showed none of the veneration for these men that was characteristic of both Coolidge and Hoover. The spending of money to promote human happiness appealed more strongly to Roosevelt than did budget balancing and meticulous economy.

Actually, the spirit of the times had changed with the same depth and breadth as had the economy. Hoover was something of a "stuffed shirt," a characteristic that had appeal in 1928. In 1932 that same characteristic was unforgivable in a public figure. Hoover could not change in response to the changes that had occurred in the nation. He was defeated. There is a paradoxical quality about leaders. The great leader is, almost invariably, an inspired follower. He must be able to reflect the spirit of his time; he must be able to divine the dominant aspirations and hopes of the population and move in that direction.

Hoover had become the scapegoat of the nation. For all his abilities, he lacked the gifts that Roosevelt had in abundance—political camaraderie, communicable personal warmth, thrilling leadership. And these were the qualities that the people of America hungered for in the depression year of 1932. Hoover now appeared dour and taciturn and was unjustly thought to be callous to the people's plight. A grim joke of the time observed that Hoover, the great engineer, had drained, ditched, and damned the country.

Although sincere and a dogged worker, Hoover was unable to dramatize his battle in a way to inspire the nation's imagination or rally its faltering morale. He was blamed for a disaster the seeds of which had been sown long before he came to office and that would have come no matter who had sat in the White House.

At no time was the difference between the two men more obvious than on the afternoon of March 4, 1933. More than 100,000 people filled forty acres of lawn and pavement before the east front of the Capitol, while millions more gathered around their radios to hear the new president's inauguration. In Washington the atmosphere that day was charged with excitement. Hoover's grave and downcast face was in striking contrast to the vibrant self-confidence of his successor, who stood without hat or overcoat in the chill wind, speaking for twenty minutes with firm voice and characteristic jaunty, almost defiant, chin.

In his inaugural address Roosevelt pledged prompt and decisive action and was able to convey some of his own unshakable self-confidence to the people who heard him. "This is a day of national consecration," he began and outlined his program in words everyone could understand. He told the nation that unemployment would be dealt with "as we would treat the emergency of war." The banks and stock market that had failed the nation would be regulated and controlled. "The money-changers," he said, "have fled from their high seats in the temple of our civilization. We may now restore that temple to the

*As Roosevelt rode back to the White House after his inauguration,
it seemed as if the champion had indeed arrived*

ancient truths. The measure of that restoration lies in the
extent to which we apply social values more noble than
mere monetary profit." President Roosevelt concluded by
saying, "This great nation will endure, as it has endured,
will revive and prosper. . . . The only thing we have to
fear is fear itself."

As he drove back to the White House after the inauguration ceremony through cheering crowds, Roosevelt
responded to the ovation by raising clasped hands over
his head and shaking them in the prize fighter's symbol
of victory. To many Americans, it seemed as if the
champion had, indeed, arrived. Like few other American
political figures before or since, Franklin Delano Roosevelt captured the imagination, affection, and respect of
the nation. For the moment people of all shades of political view were his to command.

Here, again, we see an example of the vagaries of public opinion. Several months earlier, Hoover had told the nation that "90 per cent of our difficulty in depressions is caused by fear." But whenever Hoover made optimistic statements, he was invariably charged with wishful thinking or complacency. When he admitted the gravity of the situation, he was called "the distinguished pessimist." There was nothing he could do that was right. Roosevelt, however, having inherited the national disaster from his predecessor, could face the situation boldly in all of its bleakness. He needed no personal apology and could confidently call for mass effort and sacrifice to master the crisis that had been responsible for his mandate of power.

Once the inauguration ceremony had been observed, action came swiftly and in unprecedented volume. There had been a four-month hiatus between the election of Franklin Roosevelt in November 1932 and the inauguration. During the intervening months, Hoover invited Roosevelt's cooperation in fighting the crisis. But Roosevelt refused to accept responsibility without accompanying power or to subscribe to Hoover's proposals. While a "lame-duck" president and Congress went through the motions of government, the economy reached the lowest point in its disastrous descent. Most of the country's banks were closed, industrial production was down to 56 per cent of the 1929 level, stock and security values were at a fraction of their 1929 peaks, and unemployment was approaching the 15,000,000 mark.

Franklin D. Roosevelt was the last President to be inaugurated in March. The date was changed to January in order to shorten the period between election and taking

of office. During the interim period, however, Roosevelt
was actively making preparations for his administration.
He chose a cabinet and in a series of meetings with them
made plans for the wide-ranging measures which would
make up his program. Roosevelt's cabinet reflected his
desire to maintain the support of the Republican progres-
sives who had bolted their party to support his campaign

*Roosevelt and his cabinet. From left to right: Daniel Roper,
Secretary of Commerce; Harold Ickes, Secretary of the Interior;
George H. Derm, Secretary of War; Cordell Hull, Secretary of
State; FDR; William H. Woodin, Secretary of the Treasury;
Attorney General Homer Cummings; Claude Swanson, Secretary
of the Navy; Henry Wallace, Secretary of Agriculture; and
Frances Perkins, Secretary of Labor*

and to create a balance among the many conflicting political and economic forces in the country.

His cabinet included three Republicans—Secretary of Agriculture Henry A. Wallace, Secretary of the Interior Harold L. Ickes, and Secretary of the Treasury William H. Woodin—all of whom provided distinguished service to the Democratic administration. For the first time in history, the cabinet also included a woman, Secretary of Labor Frances Perkins. The remaining cabinet members were Democrats representing liberal and conservative factions in the party and coming from all parts of the country.

In his first official act as president, Roosevelt called Congress into special session for Sunday, March 5, 1933 —one day after he took office. At this session, the President asked for and received emergency powers with which to combat the deepening financial crisis. He signed an order forbidding the export of gold and all dealings in foreign currency and another order declaring a national bank holiday. All the nation's banks would be closed to permit examination of the soundness of individual banks before their gradual reopening. These emergency measures were designed to restore the nation's faith in its currency. Without faith, currency is no more than a piece of printed paper, and this faith was dwindling fast. A barter system had occurred in parts of the country where people would not accept any currency whatever, and some states and municipalities had begun to print money of their own. Unless the value of currency could be restored and strengthened there could be no progress towards relieving the conditions of depression.

On March 9 the Congress of the "hundred days" met

in regular session to pass on the bills and emergency programs that Roosevelt had formulated with his cabinet during the past four months. All of the President's emergency measures were endorsed by an overwhelming majority in both the Senate and the House. Roosevelt asked for and got additional funds to expand the programs of the Reconstruction Finance Corporation to help reorganize the nation's closed banks and an authorization to issue more currency. By the end of the week, banks began reopening for such essentials as supplying cash for medicines, relief funds, and payrolls.

Hoover had depended upon the voluntary cooperation of business to fight the depression. He saw the stock market crash as primarily a paper debacle that could be checked by intelligent cooperation at the top. As we have already seen, Hoover called numerous conferences of business leaders and financiers. At these meetings he gained promises of increased spending from railroads, the telephone companies, and steel manufacturers and pledges of sustained wage rates and employment levels. Most of these commitments were honored half-heartedly or evaded, and some were ignored. Hoover's basic faith in the social responsibility of business was proven unfounded again and again. Roosevelt was determined not to repeat the mistakes of his predecessor. He asked for laws that would compel cooperation.

On Sunday, March 12, after completing his first week as president, Roosevelt explained the steps he had taken to the people in a nationwide radio broadcast. He asked the cooperation of all concerned Americans. This was the first of what the press was soon calling his "fireside chats." The average citizen warmed to this sharing of ideas and programs. They responded to the President's concern, and the most successful medium of publicity for the Roosevelt administration had been discovered. The fireside chat became a regular feature and Roosevelt, with the voice and personality of a radio star, was able to come into closer contact with the people of America than any other president before him. At regular intervals throughout his long terms in office, President Roosevelt reported directly to the nation in these informal radio talks.

Over that weekend, the worst of the financial crises had been weathered. Solvent banks began to reopen the next day all over the country. These initial measures taken by the new administration helped to restore confidence in the dollar, but they were not actually meant to do anything towards bringing recovery. Once this emergency was met, Roosevelt sent a series of messages and draft bills to Congress proposing the programs and measures that made up the promised New Deal. This program, passed through Congress in the historic hundred days of the new administration, represented Roosevelt's effort as President to overcome the worst effects of depression and to provide for all the different economic and regional groupings in the nation.

The principal focus of the New Deal was on recovery, though some attention was also given to needed reform. Primary action with priority over all other considerations was centered on relief. People all over the country were penniless, homeless, hungry, and even starving. Most of the state relief programs were bankrupt and had broken down. The poor had nowhere to turn.

To alleviate these conditions Congress passed the Federal Emergency Relief Act (F.E.R.A.) and voted an

President Roosevelt used his "fireside chats" to share his ideas and programs with the citizens

appropriation of $500,000,000 for its operation. Harry Hopkins was appointed administrator. Under his direction funds were made available to bankrupt states and municipalities and agencies for direct relief to the poor and unemployed.

Congress also established the Civilian Conservation Corps (C.C.C.), an organization that provided both jobs and living facilities for some of the hundreds of thousands of young men and boys who had been wandering around the country. At its peak the C.C.C. employed more than 500,000 youths in reforestation, flood control, national park work, and other conservation programs. The C.C.C. established camps in the areas where the members lived

C.C.C. workers replanting a section of the Columbia National Forest in Yacolt, Washington

and worked. Food, lodging, and clothing were provided for the members, together with a small salary, part of which was sent home to their families.

The Farm Credit Administration (F.C.A.) brought together the existing farm credit agencies into one, centralized administration. In two years, the F.C.A. refinanced almost a quarter of the nation's farm mortgages, and a corresponding bill, the Frazier-Lemke Farm Bankruptcy Act enabled farmers who had lost their properties to regain possession.

For the small home owner the Home Owners Loan Corporation (H.O.L.C.) was set up to aid the millions of home owners who were threatened with foreclosure of their mortgages. It provided for a moratorium on all mortgages and for funds to refinance existing loans. The act saved literally millions of home owners from the loss of their homes at a time of growing unemployment and falling wages.

The key loan agency of the New Deal, however, remained the Reconstruction Finance Corporation, which was established by Hoover. Under Roosevelt its provisions were broadened and extended to include loans to small as well as large businesses. Jesse H. Jones was appointed administrator of the R.F.C. by Roosevelt, and under his direction the agency lent more than $15,000,000,000 between 1932 and 1941 to all kinds of businesses. Most of this money was ultimately repaid.

Enough money was poured into the economy through these relief measures to begin things moving. As the funds seeped into the hands of the poor and unemployed and into business, the considerable purchasing power the allotments represented began to make itself felt. By early summer of 1933 there was a small flurry of excitement in the business community. Manufacturers found they could begin selling their products again and production, for the first time in almost four years, began to creep upward.

Actually, Roosevelt had not envisioned public spending as the primary role of the relief programs. He saw them as emergency measures that would help alleviate some of the terrible conditions of the poor and unemployed. In his view, they would be reduced as soon as possible to limit government spending and help balance the budget, which had already accumulated a huge deficit.

More important to the over-all economy, according to Roosevelt's own statements at the time, were the recovery measures of the New Deal. The key programs were embodied in two bills: one designed to restore farm prosperity and the other to stimulate industry and manufacture. Agriculture and industry were the main props to the economy. If these two factors could be brought back to normal, the rest of the economy would soon follow.

The first act established the Agricultural Adjustment Administration (A.A.A.) the objective of which was to raise the proportion of the national income going to the farmer. Agriculture had been the "sick man" of the national economy throughout the prosperity of the twenties. The depression merely intensified an already critical situation.

Henry A. Wallace, who was later to become a controversial figure in politics, was appointed as administrator. Under his direction the A.A.A. instituted a broad attack upon the farm problem. The objective was to raise farm prices to a level that would bring farm income in line with that of the rest of the population.

The problem, simply stated, was that the small farmer found himself in direct competition with ever-growing large-scale agricultural operations. The large operator—by using machinery, fertilizers, and modern planting and harvesting techniques—could produce at a much lower price than the family farmer who depended primarily on his own labor for production. This, together with a generally falling price structure, put an irresistible squeeze on the small farmer. It cost him more to produce his crops than he could realize through sales. It is not difficult to see the end result of this situation—bankruptcy.

In order to overcome this condition the A.A.A. proposed a "domestic allotment" scheme through which producers of seven basic farm commodities—wheat, cotton, corn, hogs, rice, eggs, and dairy products—would receive cash subsidies from the federal government in return for reducing production. The plan was designed to take about 40,000,000 acres out of cultivation. The subsidies were to be financed through a processing tax levied on flour millers, meat packers, processors, and canners. The idea behind this program was that less production would mean less supply, which would raise the prices of these commodities to a point where their production would be profitable to the growers.

Even more controversial than the agricultural price-support program were the measures enacted in the National Industrial Recovery Act (which established the National Recovery Administration, N.R.A.), by which the government assumed control over the major industries of the country. This measure was, in part, demanded by industrial and business interests as a means to control competitive practices. In a series of meetings with industrial and business leaders, the N.R.A. administrator, General Hugh S. Johnson, worked out a set of codes establishing maximum hours and minimum wage standards, abolished sweatshop and child labor in many industries, and required businessmen to open their books to government inspectors. Any violation of the code meant loss of the blue eagle (the symbol of cooperation) by the offending concern. Since the N.R.A. had received a great deal of publicity and commanded overwhelming public support, any company losing its blue eagle could expect a disastrous drop in its business.

In effect, the N.R.A. placed a large part of the nation's private industry under centralized federal control. Although the measure was originally championed by business and industry, labor also came in for its share of benefits. Besides guaranteeing minimum wage and hour standards, the act also gave labor the right to bargain with employers through representatives that they had themselves elected. The bill abolished the company union.

A third recovery measure was outlined in the Public Works Administration (P.W.A.), which was designed as a direct attack upon unemployment. With an appropriation of $3,500,000,000 for public works of all kinds, the P.W.A. was placed under the direction of Harold L. Ickes who administered the construction of vast public projects that included the dams and electrical generating and irrigation works of the Tennessee Valley Authority (T.V.A.), Boulder Dam (now Hoover Dam) at the Nevada–Arizona border, the Triborough Bridge in New York City, more than fifty military airports throughout the nation, sewage systems, civic buildings and auditoriums, and highways and roads.

Boulder Dam, built under P.W.A., was completed in 1935

As far as basic reforms were concerned, the New Deal program concentrated mainly on abuses in banking and stock market trading. The "Truth In Securities" Act was passed in late March 1933 and established the Securities and Exchange Commission (S.E.C.), which regulated stock market practices through a limit on bank credit for speculative purposes, a code which made it mandatory for the seller of a stock or security to provide the buyer full information about the company or corporation that issued the stock, and safeguards designed to prevent manipulation of stock prices.

Banking reforms passed during these historic one hundred days included the establishment of the Federal Deposit Insurance Corporation (F.D.I.C.), which guaranteed deposits up to $10,000 in member banks, thus protecting the depositor against loss through bank failure, and set up a strict code curbing speculation by banks.

Finally, Prohibition was repealed through the twenty-

These cartoons show two opposing views of the early Roosevelt days. Though millions responded enthusiastically to the New Deal programs, some feared the excessive growth of governmental power

Looks as If the New Leadership Was Really Going Lead.

THE BANYAN TREE

first amendment, which went into effect on December 5, 1933. The "wets" had finally won over the "drys," and the sale and consumption of alcoholic beverages was no longer a crime. The "great experiment" had proven to be a dismal failure. Congress realized that the morality of a nation cannot be enforced by law.

By the summer of 1933, Washington's "alphabet soup" was boiling briskly. A new spirit was in the air, the promise of dynamic leadership had been fulfilled. Millions responded enthusiastically to the New Deal programs, while a minority viewed the measures with mounting alarm. They warned that Roosevelt had overstepped the limits of government and made dire predictions for the future, but things were moving again and their warnings were ignored.

In a book titled *Looking Forward,* the President told the nation in 1933 that "We are on our way." After the years of stagnation and despair, no words could have been more welcome. The people cheered their president, and hope became possible again. Franklin Delano Roosevelt commanded the loyalty and affection of the nation as have few other presidents in American history. The first years of the New Deal was a honeymoon, a true love match between the President and the people.

For the time being, Roosevelt was irresistible and could do no wrong. Will Rogers, a popular folk comedian of the time, described the relationship between Roosevelt and the people like this: "The whole country is with him. Even if what he does is wrong they are with him. Just so he does something. If he burned down the Capitol, we would cheer and say, 'Well, we at least got a fire started anyhow.' "

THE LABOR MOVEMENT 8

If the twenties can be characterized as a decade of industrial and financial growth and centralization, the thirties may be described as a decade of growth and centralization of organized labor. In 1929 the labor unions in America counted a bare 3,000,000 workers in their ranks. By 1940 this number had swelled to more than 10,000,000. In 1929 such mass-production industries as steel and automobiles were completely unorganized as far as labor was concerned. There were no unions in these vital industries. Within ten years they were completely organized into "closed-shop" organizations in which all production-line employees were unionized.

Like the financial and industrial consolidations that occurred in the 1920s, the emergence of organized labor as a potent economic and political force in the thirties marked profound changes in the life of America. This development of two powerful and opposed forces established a structure that remains to this day and that continues to shape the patterns of life in this country.

After a brief flurry of organizational activity during and immediately following World War I, the American labor movement experienced a ten-year period of decline. Management was firmly entrenched and had a powerful ally in the government which almost invariably sided with business in all labor disputes. As long as prosperity prevailed and working people shared in its benefits, there was no pressing need for organization. Throughout this period union membership and influence dwindled steadily. It was the time of the "company union" and the "yellow-dog" contract, which bound employees from joining or organizing independent unions or workers' organizations. The low point for organized labor came with the economic collapse, which caused a further reduction in union membership and in the power of collective bargaining.

Like the rest of the nation, organized labor was shocked and bewildered by the swiftness and severity of the economic collapse. It had neither the strength in numbers nor the organizational power to act in behalf of its members. And the working people of America were the first struck by the effects of depression. In a period of declining activity, the first act of management is cutting costs wherever and however it can. The simplest means of economy is either to lower wages or reduce the work force. Massive unemployment facilitates this process. A man is unlikely to argue about a wage cut when he knows that there are dozens of people waiting to replace him at any salary. The initial effects of the depression were mass layoffs and sharp cuts in wages, and organized labor was unable to combat them.

Indeed, the effects of depression upon the labor unions were predictable. First of all, there was a sharp drop in membership. The unemployed did not belong to unions and the number of unemployed was growing rapidly. One industrialist of the time described the situation succinctly when he said, "The strongest inducement to good labor relations is a long line at the employment office." The lines at the employment offices were long and growing longer.

In order to combat these conditions effectively, organized labor needed support from the government and began to exert pressure on both the President and Congress. The first important breakthrough came with two legal victories during the Hoover administration. After a long history of agitation and struggle against employer-organized and -sponsored company unions, the Supreme Court ruled in the Texas & New Orleans Railway case in 1930 that an employer's attempt to force a company union upon its workers constituted interference with their civil rights. The decision of the court was unanimous. Although the company union was not outlawed by the decision, it was illegal for a company to force its unions upon its employees.

Then, in March 1932, President Hoover signed the Norris–La Guardia Act, which he opposed, outlawing the widespread practice of yellow-dog contracts. A company could no longer prevent its employees from organizing protective unions of their own choosing. This law was based upon the premise that the individual worker was helpless in his relationship with his employers unless he gained strength through "association, self-organization, and designation of representatives of his own choosing, to negotiate the terms and conditions of his employment."

These two developments, passed against the opposition of the administration, established a precedent that was to be broadened and extended under the Roosevelt administrations. President Roosevelt, unlike his predecessors, aligned himself with organized labor from the beginning of his administration. The reasons for this alignment were complex. Politically, labor, which included the majority of the population in its ranks, represented a potential source of unassailable power. Workers had numbers, if nothing else, and they also had the vote. Organized into voting blocs, they could dominate the political life of the country.

Roosevelt recognized this potential and catered to it to the extent that labor became one of the principal foundations from which his administrations drew support. Another factor that influenced Roosevelt's thinking was economic. His administration was committed to fight the depression. One of the main causes, economists now agreed, was the lack of purchasing power among the working classes. They had not been able to obtain a fair share of the nation's wealth. This same lack of purchasing power now acted to frustrate efforts to stop the downward spiral. People simply did not have enough money to buy the things they needed, let alone wanted. Without purchasing power there can be no demand in a capitalist economy. Where there is no demand there is a reduction in supply. The cycle could, of course, be broken by increasing the purchasing power of the working classes.

Organized labor could effect this needed change by raising wages or at least maintaining their levels.

Still another factor in Roosevelt's alignment on the side of labor was philosophical. The President's political career could be traced through his gradual drift to the left. When he first ran for public office in 1910, Roosevelt was a conservative, but this outlook changed gradually under the force of events and his own sympathies until his programs became, to many, alarmingly radical. His personal suffering as the result of paralysis, perhaps, made him more sensitive to the sufferings of others. The depression had catastrophic effects on the American people. Roosevelt was able to sympathize with the plight of the poor and the unemployed, and this sympathy led to action on their behalf.

From the very start of his administration, Roosevelt aligned himself with labor and encouraged its organization. The Hoover administration had seen the outlawing of the compulsory company union and the yellow-dog contract. Now the Roosevelt administration broadened this legislative base of labor support. Section 7A of the National Industrial Recovery Act not only strengthened the provisions of the Norris–La Guardia Act, but it also provided specifically for employees' rights to "organize and bargain collectively through representatives of their own choosing" under no management restraint or coercion.

Although it was a clear invitation for labor to organize, management attempted to utilize the legislation to multiply company unions and interpreted it as a prop for the "open shop." Labor, on the other hand, saw it as an emancipation from company unionism and was encouraged to more vigorous efforts. John L. Lewis, head of the United Mine Workers, for example, used this legislation to spearhead a remarkably successful membership drive. "The President wants you to join the union," he told miners in pamphlets, meetings, and radio speeches. Membership in the U.M.W. soared from some 100,000 in 1932 to 400,000 in 1935. By the end of the drive, there were few miners in the country who did not belong to the union.

The controversial National Recovery Administration also had important provisions favorable to workers. It established a floor under wages and a ceiling over hours that were compulsory for employers who enrolled in the program. One of the most important effects was the change in the working patterns of the country. Before this the average workweek in industry was six days and the workday ranged from ten to twelve hours. By 1936, the five-day, forty-hour week had become the rule throughout industry. In smaller towns and in the South resistance to the shorter workweek was stronger, but here too change eventually came.

Encouraged by government policies, labor unions grew in number and in the influence they were able to exert despite mass unemployment and depressed economic conditions. This new strength manifested itself in a series of sharp clashes between labor and management. Strikes of all kinds spread from industry to industry as labor attempted to shift some of the cost of depression onto management.

The government, in order to mediate between these two forces, created the National Labor Board (N.L.B.) in August 1933 with Senator Robert F. Wagner, Sr., of New

York as chairman. At first, the board had no executive or judicial powers and acted solely in an advisory capacity. This role proved unsatisfactory to all concerned, and the agency was strengthened in 1934 when Congress established the National Labor Relations Board (N.L.R.B.) with executive powers. Composed of three labor relations experts, the N.L.R.B. was set up to act as an impartial arbitrator in labor-management disputes whose decisions were binding upon both sides.

Perhaps the most important decision of the N.L.R.B., and the one most bitterly opposed by management was that against the Houde Engineering Corporation. The board ruled that under Section 7A of the National Industrial Recovery Act, an employer could not bargain with a minority but had to deal with a majority as the sole collective agent for all employees. Although there was no provision in the decision for compelling workers to join this organization, the ruling paved the way for the "closed" union shop in which all employees are members of the union and the "vertical" industry-wide union, which included a number of different crafts and job categories in a single organization.

Following the collapse of the N.R.A., which was ruled unconstitutional by the Supreme Court in 1935, and with it the N.L.R.B., labor by this time was strong enough to press for legislation to salvage its gains. In response, Congress passed the Wagner Labor Relations act of July 5, 1935, which not only salvaged labor gains of the past but broadened the rights of organized labor still further. The act forbade interference on the part of management with union organizing or collective-bargaining activities and made it illegal for management to refuse to deal with employee representatives. It also outlawed the notorious "blacklist" by which active unionists were refused employment.

As a result of the new militancy on the part of labor with the encouragement of the administration, the middle years of the decade witnessed a widespread wave of industrial turmoil. The summer of 1934, for example, saw a series of crippling strikes that reached into practically every industry in America. In Minneapolis a general strike led by the truck drivers led to bloodshed when company police tried to import workers—"scabs"—to break the strike. In San Francisco a longshoreman's strike begun in May brought sympathetic unions into a four-day general strike in July that completely paralyzed the city.

As labor became more militant, strikes became more frequent and violent. A policeman lies injured after being hit by one of the striking longshoremen on the San Francisco waterfront in 1934

In September 1934 a threatened cut in production and thus in pay brought 350,000 southern textile workers out on strike.

Another development from this period marked a fundamental change in the structure of organized labor. Before this time, labor was dominated by the traditional "horizontal" or craft structure of the American Federation of Labor (A.F. of L.), which was organized in terms of skills. Thus plumbers were joined in one autonomous union while carpenters were in another, though both were loosely related to the parent organization. Each craft union acted as an independent agent and bargained with management individually for the best terms they could win for their members.

This structure, it was felt by the more militant unionists, was outdated. Not only was it a stumbling block in the path of solidarity, since it splintered membership into separate, often competing, unions, but it also did not correspond to the industrial conditions that now prevailed. The industrial giants were all under single management while the unions were separated into craft organizations. Jurisdictional disputes between craft unions were common, and a great deal of labor energy was wasted in fighting among themselves.

Another development that demanded change was the widespread effort to organize the mass-production workers in the automobile, steel, and other manufacturing industries. Since the majority of production workers were semiskilled, they tried to organize on an industry-wide basis with all the workers joining a single union. These attempts encroached upon the jurisdictional rights of the A.F. of L. craft unions. The A.F. of L. insisted that the newly organized workers in these industries be absorbed into the existing craft structure.

Such a procedure, the new leaders felt, was not practical and would weaken the bargaining strength of the union. A single union, representing all the workers in a particular industry, it was argued, could better defend the rights and improve the working conditions of its members.

John L. Lewis, of the United Mine Workers, was one of the chief leaders in this development and he was joined by representatives from such other autonomous unions as the International Ladies Garment Workers, the Amalgamated Clothing Workers, the International Union of Oil Field, Gas Well, and Refinery Workers, and other militant labor leaders. In November 1935 they organized the Congress for Industrial Organization, within the parent body of the A.F. of L. Earlier, a start had been made towards the development of "industrial" unions with the chartering of the United Auto Workers in August 1935 and the United Rubber Workers a month later.

When the resolutions for allowing the mass-production industries to organize on an industry-wide basis were defeated at the A.F. of L. convention later that month, the eight unions that had organized the C.I.O. bolted from the parent organization. They established an independent labor organization on their own. Under the leadership of John L. Lewis, who was elected chairman, the C.I.O. instituted a broad program of aggressive organization and political activity and succeeded in winning union recognition in the mass-production industries.

The newly established C.I.O. represented a new phase in the American labor movement. Free of the traditions and methods of the A.F. of L., it developed into a force

Labor Day Amenities.

*When John L. Lewis led the C.I.O. away from the A.F. of L.,
labor emerged as an important political bloc*

for political action such as the nation had never seen. Disavowing the traditional role of labor as a more or less passive political spectator, C.I.O. activists leaped into the arena. They raised money for political candidates, rang door bells, campaigned vigorously in union meetings and on the job, erected billboards and posters, bought radio time, and molded labor into a political "bloc" of impressive strength. In the 1936 presidential elections the political arm of labor provided an important role in Roosevelt's overwhelming victory over his Republican opponent.

Labor emerged from this election as a force that could no longer be ignored by anyone seeking political office. An active participant in the political process, labor was eager to use the fulcrum of government to attain its end. The New Deal politicians, in turn, grateful for working-class support and aware of their heavy commitments to a prolabor policy, showed great reluctance to restrain union activity. The tables were turned. Where the earlier Republican administrations openly courted and favored big business, the New Deal behaved the same way toward organized labor and favored this segment of the population in many of its most important policies and decisions.

Labor, however, needed all the governmental support it could get. In confronting industry, it was challenging some of the most powerful and well-established interests in the nation. The principal objective of the unions at this time, was the organization of the mass-production industries, which fought bitterly to prevent the unions from gaining a foothold among their employees. To meet labor's growing challenge, management depended heavily on brute force. Company after company either hired private police and detectives from such organizations as

the Pinkerton and Burns agencies or organized their own
security forces. Company agents infiltrated the ranks of
the union. They acted as "stool pigeons," or "finks" in-
forming management of union plans, and strike breakers.

In many cases, management dropped all restraints in
fighting the unions. The Ford "service division"—a eu-
phemism for their privately organized security forces—
was particularly notorious in this respect, although it was
far from being an exception. Its agents beat up union
organizers and set off explosives in union headquarters.
Stool pigeons reported union plans to management, and
agents provocateurs, hired and paid by management, engineered situations where company security forces could
intervene. The unions resisted, and a wave of bloodshed
threatened to engulf the nation.

To counter these measures, the unions developed new
techniques and tactics for the struggle. One of the most
dramatic was the "sit-down" strike, where workers
dropped their tools and "sat on the job," taking physical
possession of a plant or factory. For the union, this tactic
of passive resistance had many advantages. Not only did it
prevent the company from sending in scabs to take over
jobs, but it was also more comfortable than picketing, and
encouraged a sense of solidarity among the strikers. They
got to know each other under siege and shared the dan-
gers and excitement of running the managerial blockade
to bring food and medicines to their embattled brothers.
As a tactic the sit-down strike became identified with the
great organizational battles of the 1930s.

The first successful use of this technique occurred in
1933 when the workers at the Hormel Packing Company
in Minnesota took over the plant. In 1935 workers at the

Goodyear plant in Akron, Ohio, won union recognition through a sit-down strike. The technique, however, gained national notoriety in the great C.I.O. battles with the automobile companies. Beginning in November 1936 with a strike against the General Motors plant in Flint, Michigan, the sit-down spread until it engulfed the plants of the whole company. It spread to fourteen states and involved upward of 200,000 men at its height—virtually the entire General Motors labor force. General Motors called out its security forces to evict the strikers, but the workers held fast. Then management petitioned Michigan's Governor Frank Murphy to call out the National Guard, arguing that by occupying General Motors' plants, the strikers were threatening the entire private property system. Governor Murphy, however, refused to call out the Guard, insisting that the union was acting within its rights. Instead, he offered his services as mediator in the dispute. Governor Murphy was later appointed to the Supreme Court.

Finally, in February 1937, after the striking workers had occupied the plants for four months and stopped production completely, General Motors gave in. They recognized the union—the United Auto Workers—as the sole bargaining agent for its production employees and negotiated a work contract. The other big automobile companies succumbed to the same tactics.

A more dramatic victory was won by labor in the steel industry. Threatened by a sitdown strike in its plants, the United States Steel Corporation, the largest in the industry, capitulated. It recognized the union and negotiated a work contract that included a 10 per cent hike in wages, a shorter workweek, provision for overtime pay and other benefits. "Big Steel" had given in without a fight. Encouraged by its victories in the automobile and steel industries, labor embarked on new membership drives in other areas of employment.

Organizers worked with bakers and shipbuilders; chocolate makers and grave diggers; textile workers and oil refiners; truck drivers and construction workers in a drive that reached into every industry and every manufacturing plant. After the smoke had cleared, labor emerged as a prime economic force. Big business now confronted an equally powerful big labor that could muster political strength as well as worker solidarity in its struggle for an equitable share of America's wealth.

One geographic area, however, resisted the union organization drive. This was the American South. Although industry was developing rapidly in this basically agricultural area, especially in steel, mining, and textiles, southern workers proved to be difficult to organize. Most observers traced the roots of this resistance to the institutionalized and legalized "Jim Crow" racism of the South. So long as the working people of the South were divided into two opposed groups, with one group singled out for an added measure of exploitation, the unions could make little headway. The southern white worker had his racism, but he paid for it dearly. He paid for it in depressed wages, in the poorest schools of the nation, in inadequate relief programs, and in the lowest living standard in the country. It was an exorbitant price to pay for the illusion that he was better than someone else.

During the roaring prosperity of the 1920s the shape and structure of big business was established. This was a decade of industrial growth and consolidation. It saw the development of the national chain store and centralized merchandising corporations as well as the national market. Huge industrial and merchandising complexes emerged during this period, which brought a degree of efficiency to the utilization of technical and organizational advances that raised productivity to new heights.

The depression years of the 1930s saw a corresponding growth in organized labor. Here, too, a pattern of consolidation and centralization was established that saw labor emerge into the powerful economic and political force we know today. The vertical, industry-wide organization of labor introduced by the C.I.O. rapidly developed into a vehicle that could successfully challenge business to protect and enhance the rights of its members.

American labor, however, even during the blackest period of depression was never a revolutionary force. It was then and remains today one of the principal bulwarks of the free-enterprise system. Labor never challenged the principle of private property upon which our economic system is based. It acted, instead, as an element of reform, demanding a fair share of the fruits of the enormously productive economy of America's profit-motivated system.

As a bulwark of the free-enterprise system, the labor union movement reflects both the strengths and weaknesses of such an economic organization. The prime moving force in our economy is profit, and labor accepts this principle. As a result, a labor union is like any private business in that it must look out primarily for its own interests. Its sole objective is to get the maximum in benefits for its members, just as the sole objective of business is profit. Neither business nor labor can exercise any broader concern, for once such concern is shown, the system itself must be modified. Free enterprise, whether in the form of an industrial plant or a labor union, is responsible ultimately only to itself.

Just as the economic crash demonstrated that there was no monolithic organization of capitalists, merely individual companies looking out for their own interests, so does the history of the labor movement reveal no monolithic union structure. Labor, like capital, is broken up into separate and independent organizations the individual responsibilities of which go no further than their own membership. These divisions can be seen in the broad category of labor abuses: closed unions that maintain a monopolistic shortage thereby forcing wages up for its members; "feather-bedding" practices whereby powerful unions compel the maintenance of nonproductive workers; craft unions that discriminate in their membership requirements; and unions that perpetuate outmoded work techniques and bar the introduction of existing labor-saving machinery and techniques.

This, then, is the economic and political structure that came down to us from the depression. With only minor modifications here and there, it is the system we know. On one side, there is big business, consolidated into huge industrial and merchandising empires, which has all but absorbed agriculture. Confronting this focus of power is big labor, organized into equally effective and potent unions the sole purpose of which is to win maximum benefits for its members. Between them is the government acting as an arbitrator and balance point around which consensus can be achieved. It is an elaborate, complex structure of checks and balances in which institutionalized selfishness is accepted as the principal force for progress.

RECOVERY

9

Destruction is always swifter and easier than construction. A building that may have taken years to build can be destroyed in minutes. The same thing proved to be true about our economy. After the stock market crash of 1929, it collapsed.

Rebuilding the economy turned out to be a painfully slow and tedious process. The Hoover administration began the job with a number of programs and measures designed to stimulate the economy and relieve the worst of the suffering experienced by those who were hardest hit by the collapse. Hoover's measures, however, proved to be too little and too late. His administration was not prepared, either politically or philosophically, for the trying work of reconstruction.

At the very depth of depression a new president and a

new administration came to power. With a clear mandate for change from the people, President Franklin Delano Roosevelt tackled the job of recovery with a zest and enthusiasm that rekindled the fire of hope in a despairing people. Unlike his predecessor, Roosevelt realized that drastic measures had to be used to bring the faltering economy back to something approaching normal. He also realized that these measures would create permanent and basic changes in the traditional relationship between government and the economy. The New Deal administration was prepared to take these steps and would consider anything short of out-and-out revolution to bring recovery.

Roosevelt's administration, however, had no "master" plan. It confronted a crisis and was determined to do something about it. Most of the dramatic New Deal programs were improvisational in character. They were formulated and implemented to deal with specific problems. Many were frank experiments that revealed serious flaws and contradictions when they were put into practice. The agricultural program, for example, was based on an economics of scarcity in which artificially created shortages brought about through drastic cuts in production would be used to raise prices of agricultural products. A strange policy, indeed, at a time when people in America were literally starving because they could not afford to buy food even at the lowest prices.

There was no ideological basis behind these programs but rather a philosophical sympathy towards the suffering caused by the depression. And the philosophy behind these actions was more consistent than the policies themselves. Points of strength and weaknesses in the New Deal programs, their success or failure, grew clearer as time passed. It soon became evident, for example, that Roosevelt's unquestioned talent for brilliant improvisation tended to exceed his realization of measurable results.

The New Deal, though it did much to alleviate some of the more desperate effects of the collapse, was not bringing recovery. The historic hundred-day Congress saw

A W.P.A. worker at work on the new San Francisco water system. Although such programs helped to reduce unemployment, recovery still eluded the nation

an enormous amount of legislation enacted as a result of the vigorous prodding of the Roosevelt administration. Bills and programs were passed through Congress at a furious pace, but the effects they had upon the economy were relatively minor. Relief programs prevented starvation in many cases and helped many of the nation's poor and unemployed to survive, and the huge public works projects helped to reduce unemployment and funneled needed money into the economy, but recovery eluded the nation.

The initial impact of the one hundred days had a dramatic effect, but this effect proved to be more psychological than economic. During the summer of 1933 the country did experience a measurable improvement both in production and consumption. The spurt, however, could not be sustained. By November, things had slackened perceptibly. Production levels were cut, and most of the gains in private employment were wiped out. The administration reacted with a second spurt of improvised legislation.

The improvisational character of the New Deal programs can be seen in the history of the Federal Emergency Relief Administration, which was rushed through Congress on May 12, 1933. This measure was designed to provide immediate relief to the nation's needy through direct relief payments. State and local relief agencies, which were the principal vehicles for distribution at the time, had broken down and could no longer cope with the growing needs of the unemployed. Many of the agencies were bankrupt and could not pay their workers, let alone provide anything for those on their rolls.

F.E.R.A. was organized to revitalize and to operate

through existing state and local agencies. Beginning with an initial appropriation of $500,000,000, it eventually spent about $5,000,000,000 under the administration of Harry L. Hopkins, a social worker from Iowa who had served as chairman of state relief in New York during Roosevelt's term as governor.

Provisions of F.E.R.A. called for state and local agencies to share in the financial burden of the program according to their ability to allocate funds, but no rigid formula for local participation had been drawn up. Relatively wealthy states and municipalities were expected to carry a larger share of the cost than those that could demonstrate their poverty. Thus a highly industrialized state like Massachusetts contributed vastly more to the program than a poor, agricultural state like South Carolina.

These inequities in local contributions caused a good deal of grumbling in the north. Nor was the south completely satisfied by the arrangement. Here, however, objectors argued that the government had no business filling the pockets of Negroes and poor whites with money. In some states, F.E.R.A. was looked upon as a "gravy train" conveniently provided for unscrupulous politicians. They saw to it that as little relief as possible filtered down to the needy, and when it did, they made sure that it was paid for in terms of their political positions.

Despite its shortcomings, F.E.R.A. succeeded in its basic function of providing a cushion to soften the blow of poverty for the nation's poorest segments. It revitalized local relief agencies at a time when they were in a state of almost complete collapse. In the final accounting, Washington provided 70 cents of every relief dollar spent, the states 13, and municipalities 16 cents.

In its original form F.E.R.A. was designed to get money to people so that they could buy food and pay for shelter. F.E.R.A. relief came, initially, in the form of a dole, a direct allotment of money to the poor. People who received the dole, however, complained that it was humiliating to accept money without doing anything in return. A story popular in the early days of the program told about an elderly man who, after his relief checks began to arrive, went out unasked to sweep the streets of his town, saying, "I want to do something in return for what I get."

In response to this widespread attitude on the part of people who were receiving relief money, the emphasis of F.E.R.A. relief changed. Gradually, the thinking of Harry Hopkins, who administered the program, drifted steadily away from direct help in the form of a dole, even though this was undoubtedly the quickest and cheapest method for relief, toward "make-work" programs. Once the immediate crisis had come under control, Hopkins searched about for employment for able-bodied persons on the relief roles that might foster morale. Work of any kind tended to raise the self-respect of the doer and prevented skills from deteriorating.

There were, however, serious objections from many sources raised against any make-work programs. Organized labor feared the effect of low pay for relief work on the wage levels in private industry. Business interests objected on grounds that work projects would bring the government into direct competition with private interests. Both argued that a simple dole was cheaper and more efficient in effecting relief.

Despite the protests, "work relief" won over the straight

dole as the preferred method of getting money to the poor and unemployed, and this attitude influenced New Deal policy throughout the thirties. In November 1933 as the economy showed signs of slipping again after an earlier spurt and unemployment began to rise once more, Congress passed a bill establishing the Civil Works Administration (C.W.A.) as a stopgap, work-relief program designed to take up some of the country's growing number of people who were without work. It went into operation almost immediately to meet the onset of winter and the flagging optimism that was beginning to make itself felt after the first spurt of New Deal activity.

Originally passed as an emergency measure, the C.W.A. was typical of the New Deal programs. Work relief, it was decided through pragmatic experience, was better suited to the needs of the nation than the straight dole. Federal policy, which favored the straight dole in its initial phases, now shifted its position in response to practical experience gained in effecting its programs. Roosevelt's administration was frankly feeling its way, adopting those measures that worked and scrapping those that did not. Admittedly, there was no backlog or precedent for this kind of situation, and the New Deal had to set its own rules as it went along.

The C.W.A. put some 4,000,000 people to work during the winter of 1933–34, about half drawn from the rolls of F.E.R.A. and the other half from the ranks of nonrelief unemployed. It established a thirty-hour workweek for manual laborers and thirty-nine hours for clerical and professional workers. The fairly high wages paid by the C.W.A. and its favorable working conditions often made the agency a serious competitor with the lower-paid segment of private industry. This factor, however, tended to act as a stabilizing influence on all wage levels.

In all, the C.W.A. spent about $1,000,000,000 during the span of its existence. Most of this money went towards road repairs, upkeep of schoolhouses and other public buildings, the construction of parks and playgrounds, swimming pools, erosion control, and work on municipally owned utilities.

Since the C.W.A. was an emergency measure, its organizers had neither the time nor the facilities for adequate planning. Many of the jobs created by the agency were of the most unskilled and menial kind. And while most people welcomed the opportunity to work, those who had come down in the scale from a professional or technical career to these ranks of crude labor, displayed an understandable degree of bitterness. One professional man, a forty-three-year-old engineer and the father of five children, after working for the C.W.A. for several weeks, wrote ironically about "the idea that ditch-digging was a notable occupation."

The C.W.A., however, established a precedent for work relief. The programs and projects begun under this measure were later expanded and extended by the Works Progress Administration (later Work Projects Administration, W.P.A.), probably the most ambitious example of work relief America had ever known. At its height, the W.P.A. employed not only laborers, but also writers, artists, scholars, musicians, historians, accountants, and other professionals in projects that reached into practically every area of American life.

The C.W.A. reached the end of its legislated life in the late spring of 1934. The idea behind the program, which held that work, even though it be the most trivial and unskilled kind of labor, was better than the simple dole, had made a sharp impact upon the administration and would influence all future New Deal programs.

An entirely different approach to the problem of unemployment and industrial stagnation was made through the Public Works Administration (P.W.A.). Approved by Congress in June 1933 and passed with a massive appropriation of almost $3,500,000,000, the P.W.A. was designed to stimulate industry through public works projects that would require huge quantities of material.

Unlike the C.W.A., which recruited its workers largely from relief rolls and was subject to inevitable ineptitudes, P.W.A. work was done by private concerns under contract to the administration. Harold L. Ickes, director of the program, was a cautious and hardheaded administrator. He insisted on careful inspection of all projects before funds were appropriated, and even the severest critics of the Roosevelt administration admitted that he usually got the government's money's worth.

The P.W.A. built Boulder Dam, several dams and reclamation and irrigation works for the Tennessee Valley Authority, New York City's Triborough Bridge (which had been left unfinished in 1932 because of lack of funds), hospitals throughout the country with a total of 121,760 beds, municipal sewage systems, water supply works, civic auditoriums, government buildings, school and university facilities, and many other worthwhile public works. These projects drew heavily from such major industries as Pennsylvania steel mills, Mississippi valley cement, lumber from the forests of the Pacific slopes. They also kept some 500,000 skilled construction workers

A by-product of the Tennessee Valley development was the five thousand new homes made available in the government's first model town in Norris, Tennessee

employed throughout the depression and saved literally thousands of private construction companies from bankruptcy and dissolution.

Although the accomplishments of the various administrations were impressive, they did not succeed in bringing about industrial recovery. This fact can be seen when we trace the projected curve of employment and industrial production throughout this period. After an initial spurt in 1933 indices turned down again in the fall. The administration responded by enacting more legislation, which turned the tide once more.

By autumn of 1934 the indices began to inch upwards again steadily if not rapidly. America responded to this development by giving the New Deal a vote of confidence in the 1934 elections when Democrats swept into overwhelming majorities in both the Senate and the House as well as on the state and municipal levels.

Railroads, banks, and insurance companies began to repay loans from the R.F.C. Corporations that had been deep in the red for the past five years were cutting deficits and showing modest profits. Dividend payments were resumed by many companies, and the growing influence of organized labor assured a rising wage level. Farm income rose from a low of $5,300,000,000 in 1932 to $8,000,000,000 in 1935 while the level of foreign trade almost doubled in this same period.

Critics of the New Deal insisted that the tide of prosperity would have risen far more rapidly without all of this government meddling. Uncertainty in business, they argued, was a direct result of not knowing what further measures of government interference the President might recommend. Despite the progress it had made, the New

Deal was coming under increasingly strong attack from both the left and right.

Labor pointed to the fact that despite the enormous government expenditures, unemployment in America still hovered somewhere between 10,000,000 and 12,000,000 in 1935. Both labor and business argued that recovery was still far away. Business chafed at the restraints and regulations imposed by government and was adamant in condemning the tax burdens with which the New Deal had saddled commerce. Labor complained that the New Deal was not doing enough, that progress was too slow. People were still hungry and unemployed, they pointed out, in a land where both agriculture and industry were producing at only a fraction of their true capacity.

In many parts of the country, labor and farm unrest had assumed revolutionary proportions. The Farm-Holiday Movement, which swept the granary states of Iowa, Minnesota, North and South Dakota, Wisconsin, Nebraska, and Kansas, struck at the very roots of the free-enterprise system. Farm foreclosures were prevented by force, and sheriff's auctions were turned into farces. A common practice throughout these states in the event of a sheriff's sale was for all of the farmer's neighbors to gather at the auction. They would bid pennies for livestock, machinery, houses, and land—and their bids would be backed up by shotguns cradled in their arms. Then after the foreclosed farm had been bought for pennies, it would be returned to the dispossessed farmer.

In northern Iowa, farmers dragged a district judge who had ordered a foreclosure on a farm off the bench, out of the courtroom, and into the street. Neither the sheriff nor the local constables dared interfere. Except for the fact

Neighbors would gather at a sheriff's sale to buy the foreclosed property at a pittance—and then return it to the dispossessed farmer

that he fainted, the judge might have been lynched by the irate crowd.

Farmers and workers in several states marched on their capitals to do bloody battle with police and the National Guard. Minnesota Governor Floyd Olson was wiser than most and invited them into the capitol to address the legislature, which they proceeded to do with ample and colorful threats. "Much worse than the Boston Tea Party will happen unless farmers and workers are given relief," one furious old Swede warned the Minnesota legislators.

Governor Olson, who realized that these were not empty threats, sided with the desperate citizens and threatened to declare martial law and seize anything necessary to help the people if the legislature would not act to aid them. He stood on the capitol steps and told the small army of unemployed, hungry citizens who wanted a final answer, "If capitalism can't help you and can't prevent this sort of thing from happening to the people," Olson roared, "I hope the present system of government goes right down to hell."

A Farmer-Labor Party was organized in the Midwest in 1935 advocating a program of open rebellion and boldly stating that "capitalism has failed and immediate steps must be taken by the people to abolish capitalism in a peaceful and lawful manner, and . . . a new, sane and just society must be established; a system in which all the natural resources, machinery of production, transportation and communication shall be owned by the people and operated democratically for the benefit of all and not for the benefit of the few." Governor Olson of Minnesota, who is acknowledged today as the most popular and persuasive governor in the history of the state, stood behind and supported the F.L.P.

President Roosevelt was caught in the middle. Neither a revolutionary nor a traditionalist, he sought to strike a balance between recovery and reform. On the one hand, he sought to stave off what was a real threat of revolution, on the other, he sought to modify the existing social and economic system into a more just vehicle that could bring benefits to all the people. In one of his famous "fireside chats" President Roosevelt described his attitude toward the country after a substantial part of the New Deal's early legislation had been in effect:

Different from a great part of the world, we in America persist in our belief in individual enterprise and in the profit motive; but we realize that we must continually seek improved practices to insure the continuance of reasonable profits, together with scientific progress, individual initiative, opportunities for the little fellow, fair prices, decent wages and continuing employment.

That President Roosevelt reflected the majority sentiment of the nation was made clear in the election of 1936. Roosevelt was reelected in an overwhelming victory, carrying all but two states in the election—Maine and Vermont. This led some wag to paraphrase the old political adage: "As Maine goes, so goes Vermont."

Steering a deliberate middle course, Roosevelt's New Deal brought radical changes to government, nevertheless. The old days of laissez-faire were gone. Government now assumed an increasingly important role in all aspects of the social and economic life of the nation. The entire tax structure was changed. Whereas taxation was looked on previously as primarily a means by which the govern-

In Minnesota men and women marched on the state capitol in St. Paul to demand unemployment insurance and old age pensions

ment financed its activities, the New Deal changed it into an instrument for redistributing the wealth.

Federal laws now regulated banking and the stock market, establishing stringent rules for the operation of these facilities. Social legislation such as the Social Security Act of 1935, assured a minimum income for those who became too old to work and extended the constitutional directive to "promote the general welfare" beyond all earlier interpretations.

Under the New Deal the capital replaced Wall Street as the nerve center of the nation. Government had become the largest enterprise in the country. It impinged upon the life of its citizens as never before—taxing, lending, building, setting quotas in agriculture and conditions of employment in industry, establishing new controls over highways and interstate commerce. A whole complex of new government buildings, mostly of limestone and marble, mushroomed along the principal streets of Washington, D.C., to house the new agencies of government. Civilian federal employees rose from some 580,000 in 1931 to more than 1,370,000 in 1941.

Still, despite all of the New Deal programs and legislation complete recovery continued to elude the nation's leaders. Although definite progress had been made, it was painfully slow. In March 1939, after six years of New Deal experiment and trial there were still more than 8,000,000 Americans out of work. Indeed, a sharp recession in 1937–38 resulted in a new wave of bankruptcies and an increase in unemployment.

America, however, did not exist in a vacuum. There was a world beyond our borders—a very untidy world. Depression had not been confined to the United States. It affected all of the capitalist countries of the world.

167   RECOVERY

Economic collapse in Europe was even more severe than
it had been at home. In Germany and Italy the collapse
led to aggressive fascist regimes, bent on wars of expansion. In September 1939 Germany invaded Poland, and
Europe was at war.

America, once again, was destined to play the role of
"arsenal of democracy." Industry began to tool up to meet
the demand that was certain to come as war clouds thick-
ened. The most powerful stimulant to a capitalist economy known was coming into operation. War and its
attendant construction of the tools and weapons of
destruction would do what all the programs and measures of more than six years of New Deal had failed to
accomplish.

In 1939 there were more than 8,000,000 unemployed
Americans, in 1940 that figure was cut in half. By 1941
there was no unemployment to speak of—all of the lazy
ne'er-do-wells that conservative America had worried so
much about, the spongers who would rather live on a
dole than work, disappeared. Everyone was working.

The New Deal program, however, was not the decisive
factor in bringing an end to depression. We will never
know whether or not complete recovery would have been
effected had there been no war. Certainly, the New Deal
legislation alleviated some of the worst suffering of the
depression. Jobs were provided for millions of unemployed workers, and the relief programs aided millions
more. We can speculate that given enough time the
economy would have recovered even without the stimulus
of war, but we can never be certain. War did come, and
the economy of America went into high gear overnight.
In 1941 the last of the relief programs of the New Deal
was phased out of existence. The depression was over.

CAN IT
HAPPEN AGAIN?
10

Ever since the disastrous crash of 1929 and the depression
that followed in its wake, people all over America have
asked this question: Can it happen again? The answer
must be a qualified no. No, because as human beings we
learn from experience—though there are those who would
argue this point. We know, today, a little more about the
complex operation of the free-enterprise economy than we
did in 1929. There has been growth, however modest, in
our economic knowledge. Certainly, a developing depression would not now be confronted by measures that
would aggravate conditions as happened in the years
between 1929 and 1932.

Also, there is the fact that the social and economic
structure of America is different today than it was then.
Of course, the free-enterprise, profit-motivated economy

remains basically the same, but even here important reforms and modifications have been made. In most respects, the economy today is healthier and sounder than ever before.

The most obvious difference can be seen in the existence of a powerful, well-organized labor force. In 1929 the initial impact of the depression was experienced in the form of layoffs and wage cuts by working people. This loss of purchasing power on the part of the great bulk of the population forced the economy deeper into depression in a cycle that became almost impossible to break.

Labor would no longer allow itself to serve as a cushion for national disaster as it did in 1929. At that time, the labor union movement was weak and ineffective. It could not prevent the wholesale firing of production workers and the drastic cutting of wages that proved to be one of the most serious sources of weakness in the 1929 economy. Today labor unions are too strong and too well-organized to permit the same kind of mass layoffs and firings. Labor, organized into a powerful political force, provides a prop to the economy that did not exist before the 1929 crash.

The current distribution of the nation's wealth represents another source of economic strength which could be a factor in preventing another depression. In 1929 40 per cent of the nation's wealth was concentrated in the hands of 5 per cent of the population. This lopsided distribution was a prime cause of the stock market boom and subsequent collapse, through its diversion of so much of the nation's monetary wealth into speculation. The distribution of income is no longer quite so one-sided.

One result of this more equitable distribution is that the economy is not so dependent on luxury spending. In the late 1920s, during the years immediately preceding the crash, luxury spending on such items as furs, jewelry, yachts, limousines, mansions, and the like represented an overly large proportion of the nation's spending. Such spending is necessarily erratic and undependable. It is much easier to put off buying a fur coat or yacht than it is to stop buying food and ordinary clothing. When the market for luxury goods dried up after the stock market crash a dangerously large part of national production was affected. This reaction was swiftly translated into failed businesses, closed manufacturing facilities, and lost jobs.

Another factor that acts as a source of strength in our economy today are the reforms in banking and finance that followed in the wake of the stock market fiasco. During the thirties an aroused nation demanded a thorough investigation of banking and stock market operations and the passage of laws and regulations that would prevent a repetition of the 1929 experience.

A run-away stock market boom could not develop in today's market. The Securities and Exchange Commission has been empowered with the machinery necessary to stop any such movement. It can, for example, exert complete control over margin levels in stock transactions and could, if necessary, eliminate margin trading entirely. Margin speculation was probably the single most important factor in the boom of the late 1920s.

In addition the S.E.C. is empowered to prevent pool operations and all other forms of stock price manipulation. Any suspicious movement in the price of a stock today would result in an immediate suspension of trading in that security, followed by a thorough investigation. The publishing and spreading of "tips" and rumors is also prohibited. Indeed, full disclosure of the financial and corporate structure and soundness of a company is now required on all new security issues.

The huge investment trusts have been eliminated and those trusts that do remain, the mutual funds, are carefully regulated and must adhere to rigid standards of operation. The great utility holding company pyramids, which played such a large role in the 1929 collapse, have been flattened out to manageable size, and commercial banks are no longer permitted to speculate in securities.

Government reform and regulation has also strengthened the banking structure of the economy appreciably. Federal insurance of bank deposits, most economists agree, provides the single most significant prop to our present economy. Undoubtedly bank failures were the most demoralizing factor of the depression. Hundreds of thousands of Americans saw their life savings wiped out as bank after bank failed. This cannot happen again. The federal government, itself, stands behind and guarantees the safety of the depositor's money.

With this one piece of legislation, the fear that operated so disastrously in the early thirties to transmit weakness has been eliminated. The nation's banks, of course, play a central role in the economy of any country. A weakness in this structure spreads to all aspects of the economy. Here, then, is another important factor that would tend to prevent a repetition of the 1929 collapse.

In addition to insuring deposits in member banks, the Federal Reserve System, which regulates the nation's banking practices, has also been strengthened. Today it exerts unchallenged control over the discount rates that determine interest rates for banks throughout the country, and it provides an unassailable reserve available to all banks in cases of emergency.

Other weak points in the economy have also been strengthened. The farm program provides a measure of security for farm income, thereby protecting the purchasing power of farmers. Unemployment compensation assures an income to the worker who has lost his job, and the Social Security system helps protect the income of the old and of those who are unable to work. Finally, the tax system as it has developed over the years provides an additional element of stability by acting as a constant distributor of the nation's wealth.

A capitalistic, free-enterprise economy may be flawed by serious contradictions, but it has a saving virtue. Experience has shown that it can be modified through social reform and that these reforms appear to improve the operation of the system. Today, we can look back on a period of almost twenty-five years, since the end of World War II, during which the American people have enjoyed an almost unbroken chain of prosperity. There have been, to be sure, a number of minor recessions in this time, the most serious in the years 1953–55. In this period there was a sharp drop in business levels and unemployment mounted until it reached a figure in excess of 6,000,000. Prompt action, however, on the part of the government prevented the recession from developing into anything more serious.

Still, our economy is far from being ideal. Twenty-five

There remain huge numbers of people—many of them Negroes— who exist on a bare subsistence level in America today. This is Mississippi in 1968

years of almost uninterrupted prosperity has not eliminated poverty. There remain huge numbers of people
who exist on a mere subsistence level in America. Indeed,
a congressional investigation conducted in 1968 revealed
that malnutrition is widespread among the nation's poor;
that more than one-third of our population live in housing
that is below a minimum level of decency.

The Negro population of America, as a whole, has not
shared in the general prosperity. Unemployment rates and
income levels in the Negro communities all over the
country continue to fall behind those of the rest of the
nation. Here, of course, is one of the most serious failures
of our free-enterprise system.

Until all Americans can enjoy the fruits of our enormous productive capacity and can depend on a level of
personal security needed to plan one's life, there will
remain a serious flaw in the fabric of our society. We can
see the effects of this flaw every day in riots and unrest, in
the growing number of policemen and militia called
on to maintain order, and in the frightening growth of
crime on all levels.

Our cities reflect an additional weakness. All over the
country they have been permitted to crumble. Transportation systems are a shambles, housing has deteriorated to a
point of crisis, and all cities suffer recurrent fiscal problems. Here, in the very heart of our civilization, we find
decay and neglect. Certainly another stark failure of the
free-enterprise system.

Indeed, there are critics who argue that our economy
never did recover from the depression. They explain the
twenty-five-year stretch of prosperity as an artificial result
of continued war and war expenditures. Since the end of

World War II, America has been involved in two major conflicts—the Korean War (1950–1953) and the current war in Vietnam where the United States assumed a major role in 1964–65. Although neither of these conflicts has been on the same scale as World War II, both have been enormously expensive in terms of men and material.

It was the expenditures necessary for these wars together with the gargantuan military budgets that have been maintained in between, these critics argue, that has prevented a repetition of the debacle of the 1930s. Military spending in America during this period has represented an estimated 30 per cent of the gross national product. Entire geographic areas, it is pointed out, are completely dependent upon the manufacture of the instruments of war for prosperity.

Actually, we have no way of knowing what effect a stop to war production would have on the economy. That this kind of expenditure has been a major prop under the economy cannot be denied. Most experts agree that a cut in this spending would have to be replaced by equally large expenditures in the civil sector in order to maintain our current level of prosperity.

Certainly, there is more than enough pressing work to be done to take up the slack. Our cities are crumbling. We need thousands of new hospitals and even more new school buildings to meet the needs of a growing population. Pollution control is a crying need requiring expenditures of billions of dollars.

Whether or not such a program would be undertaken, however, remains an unanswered question. Historically, Congress, which rarely questions expenditures ranging into the billions upon billions of dollars when it comes to war, becomes suddenly reluctant and economy-minded when it comes to spending federal funds for the general welfare.

The complete elimination of poverty in America, a goal every politician espouses, could be another major economic project. These challenges then, are some of the ones confronting the free-enterprise system in the United States. Few Americans doubt that we will meet these challenges. Our economic system has proven to be remarkably adaptable and resilient. It has faced and over-

The complete elimination of poverty in America is a pressing economic project today

come many crises in the past; today it confronts the most challenging one of all.

Finally, there is a flaw that is inherent in the system itself. It cannot be eliminated by reform or legislation, for it is at the very heart of free enterprise. The prime moving force in such an economy is profit, and so long as profit takes precedent over the legitimate needs of the people, so long will the threat of collapse and depression remain. For it is the hope of profit, the hope of the fulfillment of dreams of avarice that prods the enormous productive capacity of our economy—and this motivation cannot be eliminated from free enterprise short of eliminating free enterprise itself.

BIBLIOGRAPHY

Beard, Mary. *A Short History of the American Labor Movement.* New York: Greenwood Press, 1967.

Bernstein, Irving. *The Lean Years.* Boston: Houghton-Mifflin, 1960.

Bird, Caroline. *The Invisible Scar.* New York: David McKay, 1966.

Boardman, Fon W., Jr. *The Thirties.* New York: Henry Z. Walck, Inc., 1967.

Chambers, Clark A. (ed.). *The New Deal at Home and Abroad.* New York: Macmillan, 1965.

Fisher, Irving. *The Stock Market Crash—and After.* New York: Macmillan, 1930.

Galbraith, John Kenneth. *The Great Crash.* Boston: Houghton-Mifflin, 1961.

Leonard, Jonathan Norton. *Three Years Down.* New York: Carrich & Evans, Inc., 1939.

Paradis, Adrian A. *The Hungry Years.* Philadelphia: Chilton, 1967.

Peterson, Robert Trescott. *The Great Boom and Panic, 1921–1929*. Chicago: H. Regnery, 1965.

Rothbard, Murray N. *America's Great Depression*. Princeton, N.J.: Van Nostrand, 1963.

Shannon, David A. *The Great Depression*. Englewood Cliffs, N.J.: Prentice-Hall, 1960.

Wecter, Dixon. *The Age of the Great Depression*. New York: Macmillan, 1948.

Werstein, Irving. *A Nation Fights Back*. New York: Messner, 1962.

INDEX

Coolidge, Calvin (*continued*)
  election of, 16
  foreign policy, 28–29
  vetoes of, 28
Committee for Industrial Organization (C.I.O.), 141–143, 144–147
Common stocks, 48–49
Communism, 38
Company unions, 128, 133
Construction industry, 157–158
Cox, James M., 105
Craft unions, 140
Credit
  brokers' loans (1928), 44, 49
  extent of (1929), 49–50
  nonfinancial corporation, 51–52

Daugherty, Harry M., 15
Denby, Edwin, 15
Depression, Great
  breadlines, 78
  causes of, 135
  defeatist attitudes, 81–84
  effects of, 1–2, 73–78
  end of, 167
  Europe, 166–167
  Hoover's name and, 87
  the future and, 168–177
  industrial production (1932), 118
  labor layoffs, 134
  New Deal and, 113–167
    beginning of, 113–131
    labor movement, 132–148
    recovery, 149–167
    World War II, 167
  soup kitchens, 75, 87
Detroit Golden Anniversary of Light (celebration), 57
Dice, Charles Amos, 79–80
Doheny, Edward L., 15
DuPont, Pierre, 86

Economy
  cycles, 9–10, 72–73
  distribution of nation's wealth, 169
  financial organization control, 21–22
  future and, 168–177
  laissez faire philosophy, 8–9, 163
  1919–1929, 71
  1929, 71–78
Electrical industry, 43

Fall, Albert B., 15
Farm Credit Administration (F.C.A.), 125
Farm-Holiday Movement, 160
Farmer-Labor Party, 162–163
Fascism, 167
Federal Deposit Insurance Corporation (F.D.I.C.), 129
Federal Emergency Relief Act (F.E.R.A.), 122–123
Federal Emergency Relief Administration (F.E.R.A.), 152–155
Federal Reserve Board, 49–50, 51
Federal Reserve System, 114
  power of, 171–172
Fidelity and Deposit Company, 105
Fisher, Irving, 42, 57
Florida land boom, 45–48
Foch, Ferdinand, 87
Food Purchasing Board (World War I), 32
Ford, Henry, 57, 86
Frazier-Lemke Farm Bankruptcy Act, 125

Galbraith, John Kenneth, 68
Garner, John Nance, 111
General Motors Corporation, 18
  plant strike (1936), 145